CORRECT
WRITING

Form 2

D1115983

CORRECT WRITING

Second Edition

Form 2

Eugenia Butler
University of Georgia

Mary Ann Hickman
Gainesville Junior College

Lalla Overby
Brenau College

D.C. Heath and Company
Lexington, Massachusetts
Toronto

This work is a revision of *Correct Writing,* Forms A, B, C & D, by Edwin
M. Everett, Marie Dumas, and Charles Wall, all late of the University of
Georgia.

International Standard Book Number: 0-669-01627-6

Preface

TO THE TEACHER

Correct Writing, Second Edition, Form 2 is a revision and enlargement of earlier editions. Notable changes in this edition of *Correct Writing* have been made in order to meet universal needs in colleges which now find it mandatory to return to the teaching of basic grammar, punctuation, and mechanics before moving on to instruction in composition and rhetoric. With this need in mind the authors have amplified the book to a considerable degree through the addition of definitions of terms and more thorough explanations of the principles involved in sentence structure. These definitions and explanations come at the earliest mention of a term, so that students will not have to continue their study of a grammatical principle without a clear understanding of what they have already been told. Discussions which may be enlarged upon in other chapters carry convenient cross-references that point the reader to further information available on a given topic.

The format for this edition of *Correct Writing* combines the best features of a handbook of grammar and composition with a workbook of exercises. Wherever it has been possible, the exercises have been simplified to make them more than usually illustrative of the grammatical principles involved. The exposition of the various aspects of grammar and sentence structure is presented to the student in as simple terms as possible and is more extensive than that in most other workbooks. Although the discussion of many aspects of grammar is not intended to be exhaustive, information in this present book is complete enough for a student to grasp and to learn without having constantly to rely on the instructor's further discussion. The Glossary of Faulty Diction is an especially useful feature, and it is accompanied by exercises so that it may be used both for a reference and for study.

The treatment of punctuation is a distinctive adjunct of this book, since it serves as a follow-up to the chapters in which the basic principles of sentence structure are discussed. When students reach this lesson on punctuation, they will already have learned most of the rules in the lesson, which can then serve as a review of the subject instead of a listing of arbitrary rules to be memorized. There are, however, numerous occasions when it seems appropriate simply to cite a rule without attempting theoretical explanations which would defeat the purpose of the text as an elementary handbook for composition. A rule governing punctuation, grammar, or sentence structure may be susceptible to modification or exception, but it is nonetheless useful for being arbitrarily stated. If students do not know that their sentences contain comma splices, they are hardly prepared at that stage of development to explore the subtleties of such a construction.

A central point which should emerge through a student's careful use of this text is that the study of grammar and of sentence elements is of value primarily as a means of improving communication and understanding.

TO THE STUDENT

This book is a combination textbook, workbook, and reference handbook. It contains a great deal of information in the various chapters that precede the exercises. It is a workbook in which you will be able to write your answers concerning grammatical principles which you have just studied. When you have worked all the exercises as well as the Review and Achievement Tests, you will still have a convenient reference handbook in which you can check points of grammar, usage, punctuation, and mechanics whenever you need to.

Working conscientiously through the chapters and exercises of this book will put you well on your way to a mastery of grammar and usage, which in turn will help you to write and speak accurately and effectively.

Contents

DIAGNOSTIC TEST

In the following sentences identify the part of speech of each *italicized* word by writing one of the following numbers in the space at the right:

1 if it is a noun,	*5* if it is an adverb,
2 if it is a pronoun,	*6* if it is a preposition,
3 if it is a verb,	*7* if it is a conjunction,
4 if it is an adjective,	*8* if it is an interjection.

1. I have lost my *book*. ....
2. You have been working *too* hard. ....
3. *Both* Betty and Jean went to the convention. ....
4. Do *you* have a date for this weekend? ....
5. *After* the game we are going to a party. ....
6. Irene *broke* her arm. ....
7. I knew *that* you wanted to go. ....
8. *Well*, I do not know about that. ....
9. Our Florida trip was *expensive*. ....
10. The sheriff and his men searched the woods *for* the little girl. ....
11. *When* did you decide to attend the Georgia State University? ....
12. *I* was not sure how Bill would react to the problem. ....
13. Professor Wright excused me from the final *examination*. ....
14. John *recently* moved into a new home. ....
15. Graduation day is a joyous occasion for *everyone*. ....
16. Linda's arrangement *of* wildflowers won first prize. ....
17. The Beta Club *will sponsor* a tennis tournament. ....
18. *Hey*, I want to watch the end of the game. ....
19. How many books did you read last *semester*? ....
20. Either Ann *or* Sue will wash the car. ....
21. *Oh*, I understand your position. ....
22. The miners *barely* escaped the avalanche. ....
23. *Each* member of the team played well. ....
24. The violence in the movie *shocked* the audience. ....
25. *Each* of the students prepared a written speech. ....

Each of the following sentences either contains an error in grammar or is correct. Indicate the error or the correctness by writing one of the following numbers in the space at the right:

> *1* if the case of the pronoun is incorrect,
> *2* if the subject and verb do not agree,
> *3* if a pronoun and its antecedent do not agree,
> *4* if an adjective or an adverb is used incorrectly,
> *5* if the sentence is correct.

26. A group of scientists are visiting the White House.   ....
27. Every student has their favorite subject.   ....
28. I studied real hard for the test.   ....
29. My aunt baked a chocolate cake for my brother and I.   ....
30. Can you direct me to the music hall?   ....
31. Ralph did good on his theme.   ....
32. Cold weather, snow, and sleet have taken its toll this winter.   ....
33. Did you read about Zelda's award?   ....
34. Each of the members of the panel expressed their views clearly.   ....
35. Bruce is real anxious to attend the Highland games this summer.   ....
36. The boy along with his dog had already clambered into the truck.   ....
37. Neither of his daughters have an interest in politics.   ....
38. Between you and I, a successful vegetable garden is hard work.   ....
39. Newton cannot run the mile as fast as him.   ....
40. I prefer cheese that tastes sharply.   ....
41. Last weekend the bass surely were biting at Lake Hartwell.   ....
42. Sitting on the chest was a lamp and several magazines.   ....
43. The League of Women Voters announced their support of the revised constitution.   ....
44. I certainly hope that I did good on the sociology test.   ....
45. I have not heard who is invited to the reception for the ballet company.   ....
46. The media has been concerned with the lack of an energy policy.   ....
47. We feel badly about forgetting to stop for you this morning.   ....
48. Everybody is planning to bring their lunch to the committee meeting.   ....
49. Who have you asked to introduce the guest speaker?   ....
50. We do appreciate you meeting the bus.   ....

Each of the following sentences either contains an error in sentence structure or is correct. Indicate the error or the correctness by writing one of the following numbers in the space at the right:

> *1* if the sentence contains a dangling modifier,
> *2* if the sentence contains a misplaced modifier,
> *3* if the sentence contains a faulty reference of a pronoun,
> *4* if the sentence contains faulty parallelism,
> *5* if the sentence is correct.

51. I hope to get up early, study, and to leave for the mountains by noon.   ....
52. After reading the morning paper, another cup of coffee seemed in order.   ....
53. The mornings have grown chilly which is a sure sign of fall.   ....
54. To completely stop the noise of the crowd was impossible.   ....
55. The music at River Inn was soft, soothing, and I thoroughly enjoyed it.   ....
56. Margaret has only read the opening chapter of the book.   ....
57. Because his father is a lawyer, he also hopes to practice it.   ....
58. After gathering up my beach towel and magazines, the sun came out again.   ....
59. The committee which meets frequently hopes to make a full report.   ....
60. He is a boy with ambition and who has an attractive personality.   ....
61. She thinks that her job in the antique shop is more interesting than Hannah.   ....
62. Stretched out on the couch, Wilson nodded over his book.   ....
63. One cannot be sure when you will need a second language.   ....
64. To make good coffee, careful measurement is necessary.   ....
65. Her books were stacked all over the room which made cleaning difficult.   ....
66. We either plan to spend the afternoon skiing or scuba diving.   ....
67. A poem was read to the group which was very hard to understand.   ....
68. We went for a walk around the block every morning, but this soon became a bore.   ....
69. The exhausted runner almost ran the full distance before collapsing.   ....
70. By taking the pills the doctor had given him, his leg soon stopped aching.   ....
71. The man who was weeding the garden carefully stepped over the brick wall.   ....
72. After she saw my new skateboard, Maggie began to compliment me and saying that she wanted one just like mine.   ....
73. When the dog knocked over the garbage can, it was strewn all over the yard.   ....
74. Kleer-Kleen Shampoo will leave your hair more unmanageable than any other, which is saying a great deal.   ....
75. To be successful in business, ambition is definitely needed.   ....

Each of the following sentences contains an error in punctuation or mechanics, or is correct. Indicate the error or correctness by writing one of the following numbers in the space at the right:

1 if a comma has been omitted,
2 if a semicolon has been omitted,
3 if an apostrophe has been omitted,
4 if quotation marks have been omitted,
5 if the sentence is correct.

76. Rachel Suzanne and Marian have a pet gerbil in their apartment. ....
77. Shirley Jackson's short story The Lottery has a shocking ending. ....
78. Marty knowing her way around Williamsburg led the visitors straight to the Governor's Palace. ....
79. The heavy awkward knot in the rope was hard to untie. ....
80. I am planning to fly to Geneva in July however, I do not know the exact date. ....
81. Alex wants to save enough money to go to Canada for Christmas for he has always wanted to make that trip. ....
82. Johns flying lessons are progressing well; he plans to solo in about two weeks. ....
83. Did Maria mean it when she answered, I don't think so? ....
84. Remember Mildred that you are supposed to go to the dentist today ....
85. I am told that the Rotary Club meets on Wednesdays for lunch. ....
86. If I had known where to look for my keys I could have saved a great deal of trouble. ....
87. Foster asked, "How many *ts* are there in the word *etiquette*?" ....
88. The frightened puppy had its tail tucked between its legs. ....
89. I want you to understand, Helen said, why I cannot support your point of view. ....
90. Although I avoided him the whole evening he insisted on having a private talk with me. ....
91. To tell the truth I have never liked okra. ....
92. Tim taught us some wonderful sea chanteys, including Eddystone Light. ....
93. Mrs. Morris my history teacher has two children. ....
94. He heard a noise and turned to see a rhinoceros rushing toward him. ....
95. Why dont we try to swim across the lake this afternoon? ....
96. Uncle Bill while watching the television debates went to sleep. ....
97. Her latest hairdo is a hideous mess it looks like a beehive. ....
98. The used car dealer sold me a lemon and she steadfastly refuses to discuss the problem with me. ....
99. Hamilton is a member of the so-called Peanut Brigade. ....
100. The news reporter called his informant a courageous man the informant's enemies called him a traitor. ....

CORRECT WRITING

Form 2

The Parts of Speech 1

Our own language is one of the most fascinating subjects that we can investigate, and those of us who speak and write English can find pleasure in seeking to understand its various aspects. The concern of this book is Standard English and its use in contemporary writing. The study and description of Standard English, based on the thoughtful use of language by educated people, provide standards for correct writing. Although the English language is flexible and continually changing, it is possible to follow certain principles and to observe certain characteristics of usage which can make grammar a relatively exact study and one which can widen the scope of the individual in a satisfying way.

An understanding of the accurate and effective use of English is important not only for communication but also as a vital element of creative thought. Because words are used in the formulation of conscious thought, precise grammatical usage promotes clear thinking and insures logical and systematic transmission of ideas.

Knowledge of Standard English and its acceptable forms is basic to the education of all college students. Learning grammatical terms is an essential first step toward understanding what is correct and what is incorrect in speech and writing. The best place to begin this learning of terms is with the various elements that make up a sentence, elements called **parts of speech**. Any word's identification as a part of speech depends upon its usage within a sentence. The names of the eight parts of speech are as follows:

noun	adverb
pronoun	preposition
adjective	conjunction
verb	interjection

1a Noun

A **noun** (from Latin *nomen*, name) is the name of a person, place, thing, or idea. All nouns are either proper nouns or common nouns. **A proper noun** is the name of a particular person, place, or thing and is spelled with a capital letter:

John F. Kennedy	London, England
California	The Washington Monument
The Vatican	O'Keefe Junior High School

A **common noun** is the name of a class of persons, places, things, or ideas, and is not capitalized:

girl	home	dog	disgust
teacher	park	automobile	friendship
student	street	honesty	poverty

Nouns may also be classified as **individual** or **collective**. **Collective** nouns name groups of persons, places, or things that function as units:

flock	dozen
jury	the rich
team	club

Finally, nouns may be classified as **concrete** or **abstract**. The **concrete** noun names a person, place, or thing which can be perceived by one of the five senses. It can be seen, felt, smelled, heard, or tasted. Here are some examples of concrete nouns:

door	woman	scream
dress	city	snow
tree	odor	museum

An **abstract** noun is the name of a quality, condition, action, or idea. The following are examples of abstract nouns:

beauty	truth	kindness
fear	loneliness	campaign
dismissal	hatred	courtesy

A noun is said to belong to the **nominative**, the **objective**, or the **possessive case**, depending upon its function within a sentence. Subjects are in the nominative case (The *truck* stopped), objects are in the objective case (He saw the *parade*), and nouns showing possession are in the possessive case (That car is *John's*). As you can see, there is no difference in form between nouns in the nominative and the objective cases. The possessive case, however, changes a noun's form. (See Chapter 11 for a thorough discussion of case.)

A noun may be **singular** or **plural**, forming its plural generally by the addition of *-s* or *-es* to the end of the singular form (*girl, girls; potato, potatoes*).

Nouns, together with pronouns and other words or expressions that function as nouns, are sometimes called **substantives**.

1b Pronoun

A **pronoun** (from Latin *pro,* for, and *nomen,* name) is a word used in place of a noun. A pronoun usually refers to a noun or other substantive already mentioned, which is called its **antecedent** (from Latin *ante,* before, and *cedere,* to go). Most pronouns have antecedents, but some do not.

Pronouns are divided into seven categories:

PERSONAL PRONOUNS: I, you, he, it, they, etc.

DEMONSTRATIVE PRONOUNS: this, that, these, those

INDEFINITE PRONOUNS: each, anyone, everyone, either, etc.

INTERROGATIVE PRONOUNS: who, which, what

RELATIVE PRONOUNS: who, which, that

REFLEXIVE PRONOUNS: myself, yourself, herself, themselves, etc.

INTENSIVE PRONOUNS: I *myself,* you *yourself,* she *herself,* they *themselves,* etc.

The personal pronouns have differing forms depending upon whether they are subjects (*I* will help Mr. Curtis) or objects (Gene told *him* to leave) or show possession (The red coat is *hers*). These differences in form, which are seen only in the possessive case of nouns, occur in all three cases (*nominative, objective,* and *possessive*) of pronouns.

Personal pronouns, like nouns, are singular and plural, but their plurals are irregularly formed: I, *we;* she, *they;* it, *they;* etc. The following table shows the various forms of the personal pronouns:

SINGULAR

	Nominative	*Objective*	*Possessive*
1st person	I	me	my, mine
2nd person	you	you	your, yours
3rd person	he, she, it	him, her, it	his, her, hers, its

PLURAL

	Nominative	*Objective*	*Possessive*
1st person	we	us	our, ours
2nd person	you	you	your, yours
3rd person	they	them	their, theirs

1c Adjective

An **adjective** (from Latin *adjectivum,* something that is added) modifies, describes, limits, or adds to the meaning of a noun or pronoun (*strange, lovely, three, French, those*). In other words, adjectives modify substantives. The articles *the, a,* and *an* are adjectives. Nouns in the possessive case (*Martha's* book, the *cat's* whiskers) and some possessive forms of the personal pronouns are used as adjectives:

my	our
your	your
his, her, its	their

Many demonstrative, indefinite, and interrogative forms may be used as either pronouns or adjectives:

DEMONSTRATIVE: this, that, these, those

INDEFINITE: each, any, either, neither, some, all, both, every, many, most

INTERROGATIVE: which, what, whose

When one of these words appears before a noun or other substantive, describing it or adding to its meaning (*this* cake, *those* gloves, *any* person, *some* food, *which* dress), it is an adjective. When the word stands in the place of a noun (*Those* are pretty roses), it is, of course, a pronoun.

Adjectives formed from proper nouns are called **proper adjectives** and are spelled with a capital letter **(German, Christian, Biblical, Shakespearean)**.

1d Verb

A **verb** (from Latin *verbum,* word) is a word used to state or ask something and usually expresses an action (*spoke, tells, ran, argued, fights*) or a state of being (*is, seemed, existed, appears*). As its Latin origin indicates, the verb is *the* word in the sentence, for every sentence must have a verb, either expressed or understood.

TRANSITIVE AND INTRANSITIVE VERBS

A verb is called **transitive** if its action is directed toward some receiver, which may be the object of the verb or even its subject. (*David flew the plane,* or *The plane was flown by David.* Whether *plane* is the subject or object of the verb, the fact remains that David flew the plane, making *plane* in both sentences the receiver of the verb's action.)

NOTE: The term *action* should not be misinterpreted as always involving physical activity. The so-called "action" of a verb may not refer to a physical action at all: Mr. Lee *considered* the plan, Amanda *believed* Frank's story, Louise *wants* a new car. The verbs *considered, believed,* and *wants* are transitive verbs; and their objects *plan, story,* and *car* are receivers of their "action," even though there is no physical action involved.

A verb is called **intransitive** if its action is not directed toward some receiver. (*Lightning strikes. Mother is ill.*) Most verbs may be either transitive or intransitive, simply depending on whether or not a receiver of the verb's action is present in the sentence: *Lightning strikes tall trees* (*strikes* is transitive because *trees* is its object). *Lightning strikes suddenly* (*strikes* is intransitive because no receiver of its action is present).

LINKING VERBS

There is a special group of intransitive verbs which make a statement not by expressing action but by indicating a state of being or a condition. These verbs are called **linking verbs** because their function is to link the subject of a sentence with a noun, pronoun, or other substantive that identifies it or with an adjective that describes it. A subject and a linking verb cannot function together as a complete sentence without the help of the substantive or adjective needed to complete the thought; for example, in the sentence *Dorothy is my sister* the word *sister* is necessary to complete the sentence, and it identifies *Dorothy,* the subject. In the sentence *Dorothy is vigorous* the word *vigorous* is necessary, and it describes the subject.

The most common linking verb is the verb *to be* in all its forms, but any verb that expresses a state of being and is followed by a noun or an adjective that identifies or describes the subject is a linking verb. Following is a list of some of the most commonly used linking verbs:

appear	grow	seem	taste*
become	look	smell	
feel	remain	sound	

You will notice that those verbs referring to states of being perceived through the five "senses" are included in the list: *look, feel, smell, sound,* and *taste.* (Sally *looks* happy, I *feel* chilly, The coffee *smells* good, The ticking of the clock *sounded* loud, The plum pudding *tastes* spicy.)

ACTIVE AND PASSIVE VOICE

Transitive verbs are said to be in the **active voice** or the **passive voice. Voice** is the form of a verb that indicates whether the subject of the sentence performs the action or is the receiver of the action of the verb. If the subject performs the action, the verb is in the *active voice* (*Andy ate soup for lunch today*). If the subject receives the action, the verb is in the *passive voice* (*Soup was eaten by Andy for lunch today*).

TENSE

Tense is the form a verb takes in order to express the time of an action or a state of being, as in these examples: *Helen walks* (**present tense**); *Helen walked* (**past tense**). These two tenses, present and past, change the verb's simple form to show the time of the verb's action. The other four of the six principal tenses found in English verbs are formed through the use of **auxiliary** (helping) verb forms like the following:

am	is	were	have	had
are	was	will	has	been

The use of these auxiliary verbs creates **verb phrases** (groups of related words that function as single parts of speech). These verb phrases enable the writer to express time and time relationships far beyond those found in the simple present and past forms: She *has gone* to the office; Maggie *will ride* with me; You *must finish* your dinner; He *had expected* to win the prize; I *am planning* a trip.

CONJUGATION OF VERBS

Showing all forms of a verb in all its tenses is called **conjugation.** Any verb may be conjugated if its **principal parts** are known. These are (1) the first person singular, present tense, (2) the first person singular, past tense, (3) the past participle. (The **participle** is a verbal form which must always be accompanied by an auxiliary verb when it is used to create one of the verb tenses.)

---

*These verbs are not exclusively linking verbs; they may also be used in an active sense, possibly having objects, as in the following:

The dog cautiously *smelled* the food in its bowl.
We *looked* everywhere for the lost key.
Sharon *felt* the warmth of the log fire across the room.
Nick *tasted* the chowder and then added salt.

The principal parts of the verb *to call* are (1) *call*, (2) *called*, (3) *called*. The first two of these provide the basic forms of the simple tenses; the third is used with the auxiliary verbs to form verb phrases for the other tenses. The conjugation in the **indicative mood** (that form used for declarative or interrogative sentences) of the verb *to call* is given below:

ACTIVE VOICE

Present Tense

Singular	*Plural*
1. I call	We call
2. You call	You call
3. He, she, it calls	They call

Past Tense

1. I called	We called
2. You called	You called
3. He, she, it called	They called

Future Tense

1. I shall (will) call	We shall (will) call
2. You will call	You will call
3. He, she, it will call	They will call

Present Perfect Tense

1. I have called	We have called
2. You have called	You have called
3. He, she, it has called	They have called

Past Perfect Tense

1. I had called	We had called
2. You had called	You had called
3. He, she, it had called	They had called

Future Perfect Tense

1. I shall (will) have called	We shall (will) have called
2. You will have called	You will have called
3. He, she, it will have called	They will have called

PASSIVE VOICE

Present Tense

1. I am called	We are called
2. You are called	You are called
3. He, she, it is called	They are called

Past Tense

1. I was called	We were called
2. You were called	You were called
3. He, she, it was called	They were called

Future Tense

1. I shall (will) be called	We shall (will) be called
2. You will be called	You will be called
3. He, she, it will be called	They will be called

Present Perfect Tense

1. I have been called	We have been called
2. You have been called	You have been called
3. He, she, it has been called	They have been called

Past Perfect Tense

1. I had been called	We had been called
2. You had been called	You had been called
3. He, she, it had been called	They had been called

Future Perfect Tense

1. I shall (will) have been called	We shall (will) have been called
2. You will have been called	You will have been called
3. He, she, it will have been called	They will have been called

NOTE: You have probably noticed that in the future and future perfect tenses the auxiliary verb *shall* is used in the first persons singular and plural. Traditionally, written English has required this usage, but contemporary grammarians now suggest that the distinction need be made only in formal written English and that *will* may usually be used throughout a conjugation. For emphasis, however, *shall* may occasionally be needed, especially to express strong determination or invitation:

> We *shall* overcome!
> *Shall* we dance?

PROGRESSIVE TENSES

To express an action or state in progress either at the time of speaking or at the time spoken of, forms of the auxiliary verb *to be* are combined with the present participle (See Chapter 4, Section C) as follows:

Progressive Present Tense

1. I am calling	We are calling
2. You are calling	You are calling
3. He, she, it is calling	They are calling

Progressive Past Tense

1. I was calling	We were calling
2. You were calling	You were calling
3. He, she, it was calling	They were calling

This process may be continued through the various tenses of the active voice, as indicated below:

    PROGRESSIVE FUTURE TENSE: I shall (will) be calling, etc.

    PROGRESSIVE PRESENT PERFECT TENSE: I have been calling, etc.

    PROGRESSIVE PAST PERFECT TENSE: I had been calling, etc.

    PROGRESSIVE FUTURE PERFECT TENSE: I shall (will) have been calling, etc.

In the passive voice, the progressive is generally used only in the simple present and past tenses:

    PROGRESSIVE PRESENT TENSE: I am being called, etc.

    PROGRESSIVE PAST TENSE: I was being called, etc.

In the remaining tenses of the passive voice, the progressive forms—though feasible—become awkward (I shall be being called, I have been being called, etc.).

AUXILIARY VERBS *TO BE* AND *TO HAVE*

As you have seen, the verbs *to be* and *to have* are used to form certain tenses of all verbs. Following are the conjugations of these two auxiliary verbs in the indicative mood, active voice:

The principal parts of *to be* are (1) *am*, (2) *was*, and (3) *been*.

Present Tense	
Singular	*Plural*
1. I am	We are
2. You are	You are
3. He, she, it is	They are
Past Tense	
1. I was	We were
2. You were	You were
3. He, she, it was	They were
Future Tense	
1. I shall (will) be	We shall (will) be
2. You will be	You will be
3. He, she, it will be	They will be
Present Perfect Tense	
1. I have been	We have been
2. You have been	You have been
3. He, she, it has been	They have been
Past Perfect Tense	
1. I had been	We had been
2. You had been	You had been
3. He, she, it had been	They had been

Future Perfect Tense

1. I shall (will) have been	We shall (will) have been
2. You will have been	You will have been
3. He, she, it will have been	They will have been

The principal parts of the verb *to have* are (1) *have,* (2) *had,* and (3) *had.*

Present Tense

Singular	*Plural*
1. I have	We have
2. You have	You have
3. He, she, it has	They have

Past Tense

1. I had	We had
2. You had	You had
3. He, she, it had	They had

Future Tense

1. I shall (will) have	We shall (will) have
2. You will have	You will have
3. He, she, it will have	They will have

Present Perfect Tense

1. I have had	We have had
2. You have had	You have had
3. He, she, it has had	They have had

Past Perfect Tense

1. I had had	We had had
2. You had had	You had had
3. He, she, it had had	They had had

Future Perfect Tense

1. I shall (will) have had	We shall (will) have had
2. You will have had	You will have had
3. He, she, it will have had	They will have had

MOOD

Mood is the form a verb may take to indicate whether it is intended to make a statement, to give a command, or to express a condition contrary to fact. Besides the **indicative** mood shown in the conjugations above, there are the **imperative** and the **subjunctive** moods.

The **imperative** mood is used in giving commands or making requests, as in *TAKE me out to the ball game.* Here *TAKE* is in the imperative mood. The subject of an imperative sentence is *you,* usually understood, but sometimes expressed for the sake of emphasis, as in *You get out of here!*

The **subjunctive** mood is most often used today to express a wish or a condition contrary to fact. In the sentences *I wish I WERE going* and *If I WERE you, I would not go,* the verbs in capitals are in the subjunctive mood.

1e   Adverb

An **adverb** (from Latin *ad,* to or toward, and *verbum,* word) usually modifies or adds to the meaning of verbs, adjectives, and other adverbs. Sometimes, however, it may be used to modify or qualify a whole phrase or clause, adding to the meaning of an idea that the sentence expresses. The following sentences illustrate the variety of uses of the adverb:

He ran *fast.* [*Fast* modifies the verb *ran.*]

The judges considered the contestants *unusually* brilliant. [*Unusually* modifies the adjective *brilliant.*]

She sang *very* loudly. [*Very* modifies the adverb *loudly.*]

The doves were flying *just* outside gun range. [*Just* modifies either the preposition *outside* or the whole prepositional phrase *outside gun range.*]

He had driven carefully *ever* since he was injured. [*Ever* modifies either the conjunction *since* or the whole clause *since he was injured.*]

Unfortunately, she has encountered rejection everywhere. [*Unfortunately* modifies the whole idea expressed in the sentence and cannot logically be attached to a single word.]

1e   Preposition

A **preposition** (from Latin *prae,* before, and *positum,* placed) is a word placed usually before a substantive, called the *object of the preposition,* to show relationship between that object and some other word in the sentence. The combination of a preposition, its object, and any modifiers of the object is called a **prepositional phrase** (*in the mood, on the porch, of human events, toward the beautiful green lake*). You will see how necessary prepositions are to our language when you realize how often you use most of the ones in the group below, which includes some of the most commonly used prepositions:

about	between	over
above	beyond	past
across	but (meaning *except*)	since
after	by	through
against	concerning	throughout
along	down	to
amid	during	toward
among	except	under
around	for	underneath
at	from	until
before	in	up
behind	into	upon
below	like	with
beneath	of	within
beside	off	without
besides	on	

Ordinarily a preposition precedes its object, as its name indicates. Although a sentence ending with a preposition is frequently unemphatic or clumsy, it is in no way contrary to English usage. *She asked what they were cooked in* is better English than *She asked in what they were cooked.*

1g Conjunction

A **conjunction** (from Latin *conjungere,* to join) is a word used to join words or groups of words. There are two kinds of conjunctions: **coordinating conjunctions** and **subordinating conjunctions.**

COORDINATING CONJUNCTIONS

Coordinating conjunctions join sentence elements of equal rank. In the sentence *She was poor but honest* the conjunction *but* joins the two adjectives *poor* and *honest.* In *She was poor, but she was honest* the conjunction *but* joins the two independent statements *She was poor* and *she was honest.* The common coordinating conjunctions are the following:

     and   but   or   nor   for

Yet in the sense of *but,* and *so* in the sense of *therefore* are also coordinating conjunctions. **Correlative conjunctions,** which are used in pairs (*either . . . or . . . , neither . . . nor . . .*) are coordinating conjunctions also.

SUBORDINATING CONJUNCTIONS

Subordinating conjunctions introduce certain subordinate or dependent elements and join them to the main or independent part of the sentence. In *Jack has gone home because he was tired* the subordinating conjunction *because* subordinates the clause that it is part of and joins it to the main part of the sentence, *Jack has gone home. If, whether, while, unless, although, as, before, after,* and *until* are common examples of subordinating conjunctions.

NOTE: Words like *however, therefore, nevertheless, moreover, in fact, consequently, hence,* and *accordingly* are essentially adverbs, not conjunctions; they are sometimes called **conjunctive adverbs.**

1h Interjection

An **interjection** (from Latin *inter,* among or between, and *jectum,* thrown) is an exclamatory word like *oh, ouch, please, why, hey* thrown into a sentence or sometimes used alone. An interjection is always grammatically independent of the rest of the sentence. Adjectives, adverbs, and occasionally other parts of speech become interjections when used as independent exclamations (*good! horrible! fine! what! wait!*).

Exercise 1   NOUNS AND PRONOUNS

Write in the first blank at the right any *italicized* word that is a noun and in the second any
that is a pronoun.

	NOUN	PRONOUN
EXAMPLE: *Someone* forgot to close *the gate*.	gate	someone
1. *We* took *three* rolls of *film* during our vacation.	film	we
2. Come early if *you* want *supper*.	supper	you
3. *I* listened carefully to *every word* the professor said.	word	I
4. The reporter *asked her* for an *interview*.	interview	her
5. *Everyone* values *success* in his own way.	success	Everyone
6. *He* is a *friendly individual*.	friendly	he
7. The professor gave *me* my *examination* early.		me
8. *Some students* like to study by *themselves*.	students	themselves
9. Did *you understand* his *question*?	question	you
10. *I missed* the five o'clock *train* yesterday.	train	I
11. Saving *money* is *difficult* for *him*.	difficult	him
12. *These* are the *suggestions for* the party.	suggestion	these
13. *What* is the telephone number of the *hospital*?	hospital	what
14. Norrine took *me* for a *ride* on her *new* motorcycle.	ride	me
15. *Everybody* loves the *zoo*.	zoo	Everybody
16. *Who* broke the *glass bowl*?	glass	who

13

17. The *jury* said *he* was *not* guilty.

        jury   *he*

18. Jamie *went* with *me* to the *Kentucky Derby*.

        Kentucky   *me*

19. Bob has a *friend who traveled* through Mexico on a bicycle.

        friend   *who*

20. *Bill* made *me* a model airplane *for* Christmas.

        Bill   *me*

Exercise 2   PRONOUNS

In the sentences below identify the *italicized* pronouns by writing one of the following abbreviations in the space at the right:

P for personal,   *Inter* for interrogative,
D for demonstrative,   *Inten* for intensive,
I for indefinite,   *Ref* for reflexive.
Rel for relative,

EXAMPLE: Where have *you* been?   ..... *P* .....

1. *Who* has read *Zen and the Art of Motorcyle Maintenance*?   ..... *Inte* .....

2. *We* regretted that you could not come.   ..... *P* .....

3. *Everyone* is ready.   ..... *I* .....

4. I *myself* selected the gift.   ....

5. I could not make *myself* work the problem.   ....

6. They had prepared a plan by *themselves*.   ....

7. *These* are my favorite flowers.   ....

8. Irene asked *us* to wait.   ....

9. Students *who* fail have usually not studied.   ....

10. Tipper said that he could not tell *anyone* his secret.   ....

11. He earned a reputation *which* ruined his career.   ....

12. *That* is a serious accusation to make.   ....

13. *What* is your family bringing to the picnic?   ....

14. If you apply *yourself*, you will succeed.   ....

15. Neither my brother nor *I* can attend the reunion.   ....

16. Where did you buy *those*?   ....

17. Jimmy can manage *it* quite well.   ....

15

18. Jane received all the help that *she* needed.   ....

19. *What* should I do?   ....

20. This was *something* that he could not understand.   ....

Exercise 3 ADJECTIVES AND ADVERBS

In the following sentences underline once all the adjectives and words used as adjectives except the articles *a, an,* and *the*. Underline all adverbs twice.

EXAMPLE: She is very stubborn.

1. Jake wore a light blue suit.

2. We seriously considered every suggestion.

3. The main dish was a very large salad.

4. Jan recently bought a new truck.

5. A small-town student often feels lost in a university.

6. The old man quietly entered the room.

7. In a big city driving is very often dangerous.

8. Autumn leaves are always beautiful.

9. The father spoke softly to the little children.

10. I live in a high-rise apartment only two blocks from the college.

11. He has extremely bad manners.

12. Hilda makes fresh bread daily.

13. The biology professor carefully explained the test.

14. Many citizens complained loudly.

15. She works actively with the tennis team.

16. He suddenly lost his balance.

17. He seldom goes to a soccer game.

18. The afternoon traffic moves slowly.

19. He wandered blindly down the busy street.

20. The practical student carefully plans ahead.

Exercise 4   VERBS

In the first column at the right, write the verbs in the following sentences. In the second column write *A* if the verb is in the active voice, *P* if it is in the passive voice. In the last column write *T* if the verb is transitive, *I* if it is intransitive.

	VERB	A/P	T/I
EXAMPLE: Mary was elected president.	*was elected*	*P*	*T*
1. Sam baked a cake.			
2. Henry is angry.			
3. The argument became violent.			
4. Celestine lives quietly in her old mountain cabin.			
5. The artist has not achieved success.			
6. The train will remain empty until tomorrow.			
7. I can see no way around the difficulty.			
8. Paula was admitted to the Mercer University Law School.			
9. He refused the fraternity's invitation to membership.			
10. The Appaloosa horse is one of the world's oldest breeds.			
11. They are at their best in a social situation.			
12. The coach had been given a trophy by the team.			
13. The lazy professor was brought before the board.			
14. The wildcat has finally been caught.			
15. Marge wanted a car for graduation.			

16. We must become aware of our
    responsibilities.   ....

17. Reading enlarges one's horizon.   ....

18. We drove carefully through the snow. ....

19. Our definition of leadership definitely
    excludes the gang leader.   ....

20. I stood up and slowly moved toward the
    door.   ....

Exercise 5   PREPOSITIONS

Write the prepositions in the following sentences in the spaces of the first column to the right. Write the objects of the prepositions in the second column. If a sentence contains no preposition, leave the spaces blank.

	PREP.	OBJECT
EXAMPLE: Mario is among my many friends.	among	friends
1. Do not throw the ball in the house.		
2. The professor read a poem to us.		
3. The conservative is usually against any changes.		
4. The final choice was between Frank and Clyde.		
5. Betsy stumbled down the stairs.		
6. Everyone went home except me.		
7. We planted twenty acres of soybeans.		
8. Once in the apartment, I felt safe.		
9. Our cat chased Ed's dog around the house.		
10. Mrs. Jefferson had a long talk with her son's teacher.		
11. Before the race the drivers were tense.		
12. My supervisor said that she was pleased with my work.		
13. The traffic helicopter flies over the city every day.		
14. Everyone asked questions but me.		
15. The little girl hid behind the tree.		
16. The speaker's criticism was aimed at the school board.		

17. Walking through the woods is a delightful
    experience.   ....

18. He made his confession under stress.   ....

19. Do you know anything about physics?   ....

20. I recently moved to Split Silk, Georgia.   ....

Exercise 6   CONJUNCTIONS

In the following sentences there are both coordinating and subordinating conjunctions. Write the conjunction in the space at the right, and after it write *C* if it joins sentence elements of equal rank or *S* if it joins unequal elements.

EXAMPLE: Both the faculty and the students were frustrated by the regulations.

.... *Both...and, C* ....

1. Last summer I read *The Lives of a Cell* and *The Ascent of Man.*   ....

2. When the snow melts, there will be flooding.   ....

3. Shakespeare is a writer with wit and imagination.   ....

4. As the sailor walked toward the village, he saw his ship in port.   ....

5. If you have never been to San Francisco, you will be quite enchanted.   ....

6. When Peter stayed here, he wanted his own room.   ....

7. He did not like the movie, nor did I.   ....

8. The people were delighted because they had an heir to the throne.   ....

9. Before I could answer the door, the stranger rushed in.   ....

10. Although the night air was chilly, we slept outside.   ....

11. I came because I was worried about you.   ....

12. Please wait for me at the hotel until I call.   ....

13. If I call you tomorrow, perhaps we can have lunch together.   ....

14. Irene thought that you had left.   ....

15. I can go, or I can stay here.   ....

16. Although he lost the race, he will always remember the challenge.   ....

17. I do not have the time to go, but Wayne is going.   ....

18. Before you walk to the store, make a grocery list.   ....

19. When the ground dries, I will plow my garden.   ....

20. Both you and I will attend the meeting.   ....

Exercise 7   REVIEW OF PARTS OF SPEECH

In the following sentences identify the part of speech of each *italicized* word by writing one of the following abbreviations in the space at the right:

N for noun,   *Adv* for adverb,
V for verb,   *Prep* for preposition,
P for pronoun,   *C* for conjunction,
Adj for adjective,   *I* for interjection.

EXAMPLE: Those books are *mine*.   *P*

1. New York taxicab drivers are a unique *group* of people.   ....

2. *After* a moment, the crowd stepped aside.   ....

3. *Oh*, that will be very good.   ....

4. As she waited patiently, *she* remembered only the good times. ....

5. According to the gossip, the owner was indeed *eccentric*.   ....

6. The pyramids are an example of *Egyptian* architecture.   ....

7. Leon seemed thinner *and* paler than usual.   ....

8. She turned *abruptly* and walked off.   ....

9. The *outside* of the house needs painting.   ....

10. The man *with* the beard moved cautiously toward the door.   ....

11. The children are waiting *outside*.   ....

12. I *have finished* reading her latest novel.   ....

13. *We* visited Magnolia Gardens this spring.   ....

14. My grandparents used an *old-fashioned* icebox.   ....

15. The soccer clinic will be *jointly* sponsored by J and J Sporting Goods and the recreation department.   ....

16. The Morgan horse *is known* for its endurance.   ....

17. I enjoy the beauty of the *countryside*.   ....

18. *What*, have you lost your keys?   ....

19. *When* Beverly Sills appeared on stage, the audience gave her a standing ovation.   ....

20. *Neither* his home *nor* his barn is painted.   ....

Exercise 8   REVIEW OF PARTS OF SPEECH

In the following sentences identify the part of speech of each *italicized* word by writing one of the following abbreviations in the space at the right:

N for noun,	*Adv* for adverb,
V for verb,	*Prep* for preposition,
P for pronoun,	*C* for conjunction,
Adj for adjective,	*I* for interjection.

EXAMPLE: I found *myself* unable to cope with the situation.   *P*
....

1. You must stay *outside* the house.   ....

2. The trapped animal freed *itself*.   ....

3. I enjoyed reading the book, *but* I did not see the movie.   ....

4. I have several pieces of Steve Blair's *pottery*.   ....

5. Sam made *himself* a wheelbarrow.   ....

6. If we have a garden next summer, we will build a *compost* box.   ....

7. *Did* you *see* the game between Marquette and the University of North Carolina?   ....

8. *Oh*, I can hardly wait for spring vacation.   ....

9. An Italian artist painted "The Adoration *of* the Magi."   ....

10. I think that I brought the *wrong* key.   ....

11. *Everyone* is working hard on the project.   ....

12. The rain *stopped* before we got up.   ....

13. For a moment he could *not* remember where he was.   ....

14. He scarcely noticed *me*.   ....

15. They stared at each other for several *minutes*.   ....

16. Wayne apologized *for* his remark.   ....

17. *Neither* his friends *nor* his enemies believed his story.   ....

18. *Ah!* Now I understand why you were late. ....

19. Despite the warning, the man *moved* toward the door. ....

20. Existentialism is probably the *most* popular philosophy of our time. ....

Recognizing Subjects, Verbs, and Complements

2

2a The Sentence

A **sentence** is made up of single parts of speech combined into a pattern which expresses a complete thought. In other words, a sentence is a group of words that expresses a complete thought. In its simplest form this complete statement is an independent clause or a **simple sentence.**

2b Subject and Predicate

Every simple sentence must have two basic elements: (1) the thing we are talking about, and (2) what we say about it. The thing we are talking about is called the **subject**, and what we say about it is called the **predicate**. The subject is a noun, a pronoun, or some other word or group of words used as a noun. The essential part of the predicate is a verb—a word which tells something about the subject. It tells that the subject *does* something or that something *is true* of the subject. Therefore, a subject and a verb are the fundamental parts of every sentence. In fact, it is possible to express meaning with just these two elements:

> Pilots fly.
> Flowers bloom.

In each example the verb says that the subject does something. The sentences are about pilots and flowers. What does each do? The pilots fly; the flowers bloom.

2c Finding the Verb

Finding verbs and subjects of verbs in a sentence is the first step in determining whether or not a group of words expresses a complete thought. Therefore, look first for the verb, the most important word in the sentence, and then for its subject.

The verb may sometimes be difficult to find. It may come anywhere in the sentence; for instance, it may precede the subject, as in some interrogative sentences (*Where is my pencil?*). It may consist of a single word or a group of two or more words; it may have other words inserted within the verb phrase; it may be combined with the negative *not* or with a contraction of *not*. To find the verb, however, look for the word or group of words that expresses an action or a state of being. In the following sentences the verbs are in italics:

My friend *stood* by me. [The verb *stood* follows the subject *friend.*]

By me *stood* my friend. [The verb *stood* precedes the subject *friend.*]

My friend *was standing* by me. [The verb *was standing* consists of two words.]

My friend *cannot stand* by me. [The verb *can* is combined with the negative adverb *not,* which is not part of the verb.]

Did my friend *stand* by me? [The verb *did stand* is divided by the subject.]

2d Finding the Subject

Sometimes finding the subject may also be difficult, for, as we have just seen, the subject does not always come immediately before the verb. Often it comes after the verb; often it is separated from the verb by a modifying element. Always look for the noun or pronoun about which the verb asserts something and disregard intervening elements:

Many of the children *come* to the clinic. [A prepositional phrase comes between the subject and the verb.]

There *are flowers* on the table. [The subject comes after the verb. The word *there* is never a subject; in this sentence it is an *expletive,* an idiomatic introductory word.]

In the room *were* a *cot* and a *chair.* [The subject comes after the verb.]

In an imperative sentence, a sentence expressing a command or a request, the subject *you* is usually implied rather than expressed. Occasionally, however, the subject *you* is expressed:

Come in out of the rain.

Shut the door!

You play goalie.

Either the verb or the subject or both may be **compound**; that is, there may be more than one subject and more than one verb:

The *boy* and the *girl* played. [Two subjects.]

The boy *worked* and *played.* [Two verbs.]

The *boy* and the *girl worked* and *played.* [Two subjects and two verbs.]

In the first sentence the compound subject is *boy* and *girl.* In the second sentence there is a compound verb, *worked* and *played.* In the third sentence both the subject and the verb are compound.

2e Complements

Thus far we have discussed two functions of words: that of nouns and pronouns as subjects and that of verbs as predicates.

A third function of words which we must consider is that of completing the verb. Nouns, pronouns, and adjectives are used to complete verbs and are called **complements**. A complement may be a **direct object**, an **indirect object**, a **predicate noun** or **pronoun**, a **predicate adjective**, an **objective complement**, or a **retained object**.

A **direct object** is a noun or noun equivalent which completes the verb and receives the action expressed in the verb:

> The pilot flew the plane. [*Plane* is the direct object of *flew*. Just as the subject answers the question "*who*?" or "*what*?" before the verb (Who flew?), so the direct object answers the question "*whom*?" or "*what*?" after the verb (Flew what?).]

An **indirect object** is a word (or words) denoting the person or thing indirectly affected by the action of a transitive verb. It is the person or thing to which something is given or for which something is done. Such words as *give, offer, grant, lend, teach,* etc., represent the idea of something done for the indirect object:

> We gave *her* the book. [*Her* is the indirect object of *gave*. The indirect object answers the question "*to (for) whom or what*?" after the verb *gave* (Gave to whom?).]

Certain verbs that represent the idea of taking away or withholding something can also have indirect objects:

> The judge *denied him* the opportunity to speak in his own defense.
>
> Father *refused Frances* the use of the car.

A **predicate noun** (also called **predicate nominative**) is a noun or its equivalent which renames or identifies the subject and completes such verbs as *be, seem, become,* and *appear* (called linking verbs):

> The woman is a *doctor*. [The predicate noun *doctor* completes the intransitive verb *is* and renames the subject *woman*.]
>
> My best friends are *she* and her *sister*. [The predicate pronoun *she* and the predicate noun *sister* complete the intransitive verb *are* and rename the subject *friends*.]
>
> Mary has become a *pilot*. [The predicate noun *pilot* completes the intransitive verb *has become* and renames the subject *Mary*.]

A **predicate adjective** is an adjective which completes a linking verb and describes the subject:

> The man seems *angry*. [The predicate adjective *angry* completes the intransitive verb *seems* and describes the subject *man*.]

An **objective complement** is a noun or an adjective which completes the action expressed in the verb and refers to the direct object. If it is a noun, the objective complement is in a sense identical with the direct object; if it is an adjective, it describes or limits the direct object. It occurs commonly after such verbs as *think, call, find, make, consider, choose,* and *believe:*

> Jealousy made Othello a *murderer*. [The objective complement *murderer* completes the transitive verb *made* and renames the direct object *Othello*.]
>
> She thought the day very *disagreeable*. [The objective complement *disagreeable* is an adjective which describes the direct object *day*.]

A **retained object** is a noun or noun equivalent which remains as the object when a verb which has both a direct and an indirect object is put into the passive voice. The other object becomes the subject of such a verb. Although either object may become the subject, the indirect object more commonly takes that position, and the direct object is retained:

> The board granted him a year's leave of absence.
> He was granted a year's leave of absence.
>
> [In the second sentence the verb has been put into the passive voice, the indirect object of the first sentence has become the subject of the second, and the direct object has been retained.]
>
> The teacher asked the student a difficult question.
> A difficult question was asked the student.
>
> [In the second sentence the verb has been put into the passive voice, the direct object of the first sentence has become the subject of the second, and the indirect object has been retained.]

Exercise 9   SUBJECTS AND VERBS

In each of the following sentences underline the subject once and its verb twice. Then copy
the subject on the first line and the verb on the second line at the right of the sentence.

	SUBJECT	VERB
EXAMPLE: Students <u>are encouraged</u> through discussions with their academic advisors.	*Students*	*are encouraged*
1. After colliding with an iceberg, the *Titanic* sank.		
2. Have you ever ridden on a snowplow?		
3. The blue sky turned a soft gray.		
4. Self-discipline is an admirable character trait.		
5. Lynn was chosen hockey captain.		
6. A group of students from Gainesville Junior College will tour Greece this summer.		
7. According to Keats, "a thing of beauty is a joy forever."		
8. These suggestions are timely and stimulating.		
9. Despite the warning, the strikers left the plant.		
10. Why do you want pickles in your salad?		
11. In earlier days a man's word was his bond.		
12. Any successful business needs satisfied customers.		
13. I appreciate your help and advice.		
14. Jake returned to his hotel room quite late.		
15. In the cabin were two beds, a chair, and a table.		
16. The specimens were examined by the biology students.		
17. My mother and I have season tickets to the opera.		

18. Neither the student nor the professor was happy about the test grades. ....

19. Arlie, in the meantime, will help you. ....

20. Shari's mother lit the Sabbath candles. ....

21. New courses will be added and others changed during the school year. ....

22. Tommy, as well as his three sons, attended the NCAA tournament in St. Louis. ....

23. Ed patiently waited for Jan. ....

24. I hurried to class but forgot my books. ....

25. Part of the blame is yours. ....

26. There are several pieces of fruit on the table. ....

27. Where did you find my book? ....

28. The mayor and the union met every day last week. ....

29. Earl, in the beginning, agreed with the politicians. ....

30. Have you visited the Peabody Museum? ....

31. Duke University is planning an alumni party. ....

32. A number of student leaders were present. ....

33. The committee took action last Monday. ....

34. War movies draw large crowds. ....

35. He was temporarily suspended from class. ....

Exercise 10   SUBJECTS AND VERBS

In each of the following sentences underline the subject(s) once and their verb(s) twice. Then copy the subject(s) in the first column and the verb(s) in the second column at the right of the sentence. Use only as many lines as are needed.

	SUBJECT(S)	VERB(S)
EXAMPLE: Kyle visited Israel and learned about his ancestors.	*Kyle*	*visited*
		learned
1. The Seacrest Inn overlooks the rugged Maine Coast.		
2. His attitude and work have been criticized.		
3. Rue and her family go to Atlantic City every spring.		
4. My nephew broke his arm and could not play baseball.		
5. Are you and Frances going to Canada this year?		
6. John and I are having a grand time.		
7. I stood in the rain and waited for the bus.		
8. We will leave early in the morning and return late Sunday.		

9. Hockey and soccer are my favorite sports.   ....

....

10. Both the bus driver and the driver of the car were at fault.   ....

....

11. Ralph patted the little dog.   ....

....

12. A college education is priceless but expensive.   ....

....

13. Neither the President nor the Dean is on campus.   ....

....

14. We are having problems with our hand tiller.   ....

....

15. Did you plant corn this year?   ....

....

16. Tobacco is a major crop in North Carolina.   ....

....

17. Andy and his friends spent a week at the beach.   ....

....

18. The carpenter cut each plank carefully.   ....

....

19. Baylor University has an excellent academic program.   ....

....

20. I am late for my dental appointment.

21. My sister hates country and western music.

22. Our class is planning an overnight trip to the mountains.

23. What have you done with my sunglasses?

24. Our term papers are due next week.

25. The police and the parents understand our problems.

26. Lois hurried to the meeting.

Exercise 11   DIRECT OBJECTS AND PREDICATE NOUNS

In each of the following sentences underline the complement. In the blank space write *DO* if the complement is a direct object and *PN* if it is a predicate noun.

EXAMPLE: Dr. Hammock is a psychology <u>professor</u>.   *PN*
....

1. I paid my lab fee yesterday.   ....

2. Will you give me her address?   ....

3. Tommy has become a vegetarian.   ....

4. We are planning a summer tour of Australia.   ....

5. The new chef prepared a delicious dinner.   ....

6. The weather was the cause of the airplane crash.   ....

7. What action do you suggest?   ....

8. The boy by the door is my brother.   ....

9. The film was a chilling tale of murder.   ....

10. Eudora Welty read a selection from her works.   ....

11. Have you hiked the Appalachian Trail?   ....

12. I am a stockholder in a large aircraft corporation.   ....

13. Sarah played tennis Saturday.   ....

14. Warren is an accountant with Arthur Andersen and Company.   ....

15. He solved the problem.   ....

16. Sugar does not have any food value.   ....

17. Max Ernst is a prominent American landscape artist.   ....

18. Everyone knows her.   ....

19. Will Merle become president?   ....

20. Angie will cultivate the garden tomorrow.   ....

21. She is her father's favorite child. ....

22. My only exercise is tennis. ....

23. Henry has been our secretary for some time. ....

24. I watched the game on television. ....

25. The coach's daughter is a natural athlete. ....

Exercise 12   INDIRECT OBJECTS AND OBJECTIVE COMPLEMENTS

In each of the following sentences identify the *italicized* complement by writing in the space at the right one of the following abbreviations:

IO if it is an indirect object
OC if it is an objective complement

EXAMPLE: The Rabbi read the *children* stories from the Bible.   *IO*

1. The class elected Joseph *president.*   ....

2. He sent *me* his recipe for chocolate mousse.   ....

3. I bought *you* a new CB radio.   ....

4. Did Roger paint his house *purple*?   ....

5. Lynn wrote *me* a letter explaining her new job.   ....

6. Becky cannot find her *classmates* an apartment.   ....

7. The professor considered her logic *faulty*.   ....

8. Did you bring *him* his coat?   ....

9. Our book club selected Joyce Carol Oates *author* of the year.   ....

10. Did you give the *kittens* any milk?   ....

11. Smith College mailed *Kyle* a catalogue.   ....

12. The audience gave *Marilyn Horne* a standing ovation.   ....

13. She wanted her wedding dress *simple*.   ....

14. The governor appointed Mr. Oxford a *Regent*.   ....

15. Karl won the *family* a trip to Hawaii.   ....

16. The faculty presented *Dr. Butler* a first edition of Faulkner's masterpiece.   ....

17. The blind student is teaching *us* Braille.   ....

18. Mary Jane ordered her *husband* a Porsche for an anniversary present.   ....

19. The Dean thought the faculty member *insubordinate*.   ....

20. Jane considered her sister very *selfish*.   ....

Exercise 13   COMPLEMENTS

A. In each of the following sentences identify the *italicized* word by writing one of the
following abbreviations in the space at the right:

PN if it is a predicate noun,   IO if it is an indirect object,
PA if it is a predicate adjective,   OC if it is an objective complement.
DO if it is a direct object,

EXAMPLE: The desire to travel made Ulysses *restless.*   *OC*

1. I recently reread C. S. Lewis's *The Screwtape Letters.*   ....

2. He buried his *head* in his hands.   ....

3. The young man was too *faint* and *dizzy* to protest.   ....

4. Newman is my little brother's *name.*   ....

5. Her mouth was *dry* with fear and tension.   ....

6. Did the hockey team elect *Grace* co-captain?   ....

7. He weighed his *words* carefully.   ....

8. I thought the president's speech *insulting.*   ....

9. They sent *Aubrey* to Washington.   ....

10. We gave *Jimmy* the room upstairs.   ....

11. Paula has always been a *leader.*   ....

12. The outfielder quickly threw the first *baseman* the ball.   ....

13. Threepio is a delightful *robot.*   ....

14. I found his conversation quite *boring.*   ....

15. I will read *you* a story about the magic land of Narnia.   ....

B.   Write sixteen sentences, four of which contain direct objects; four, indirect objects; four, predicate nouns; four, predicate adjectives. In the space at the right, write *DO* (direct object), *IO* (indirect object), *PN* (predicate noun), or *PA* (predicate adjective) as the case may be.

1. ....

2. ....

3. ....

4. ....

5. ....

6. ....

7. ....

8. ....

9. ....

10. ....

11. ....

12. ....

13. ....

14. ....

15. ....

16. ....

The Sentence Fragment 3

3a Grammatical Fragments

If you are not careful to have both a subject and a predicate in your sentences, you will write sentence fragments instead of complete sentences. Observe, for example, the following:

A tall, distinguished-looking gentleman standing on the corner in a pouring rain.

Standing on the corner in a pouring rain and shielding himself from the deluge with a a large umbrella.

The first of these groups of words is no more than the subject of a sentence or the object of a verb or preposition. It may be part of such a sentence, for example, as *We noticed a tall, distinguished-looking gentleman standing on the corner in a pouring rain.* The second group is probably a modifier of some kind, the modifier of a subject, for instance: *Standing on the corner in a pouring rain and shielding himself from the deluge with a large umbrella, a tall, distinguished-looking gentleman was waiting for a cab.*

Another type of fragment is seen in the following illustrations:

Because I had heard all that I wanted to hear and did not intend to be bored any longer.

Who was the outstanding athlete of her class and also the best scholar.

Although he had been well recommended by his former employers.

Each of these groups of words actually has a subject and a predicate, but each is still a fragment because the first word of each is a subordinating element and clearly indicates that the thought is incomplete, that the thought expressed depends upon some other thought. Such fragments are subordinate parts of longer sentences like the following:

I left the hall because I had heard all that I wanted to hear and did not intend to be bored any longer.

The valedictorian was Alice Snodgrass, who was the outstanding athlete of her class and also the best scholar.

He did not get the job although he was well recommended by his former employers.

3b Permissible Fragments

A sentence fragment is usually the result of ignorance or carelessness. It is the sign of an immature writer. But, on the other hand, much correct spoken and written English contains perfectly proper fragments of sentences. The words *yes* and *no* may stand alone, as may other words and phrases in dialogue; there is nothing wrong, for example, in such fragments as the following:

The sooner, the better.

Anything but that.

Same as before.

Interjections and exclamatory phrases may also stand alone as independent elements. The following fragments are correct:

Ouch!

Tickets, please!

Not so!

3c Stylistic Fragments

There is another kind of fragment of rather common occurrence in the writing of some of the best authors. It is the phrase used for realistic or impressionistic effect, the piling up of words or phrases without any effort to organize them into sentences: "The blue haze of evening was upon the field. Lines of forest with long purple shadows. One cloud along the western sky partly smothering the red." This kind of writing, if it is to be good, is very difficult. Like free verse, it may best be left to the experienced writer. Students should learn to recognize a sentence fragment when they see one. They should use this form sparingly in their own writing. And they should remember two things: first, that the legitimacy of the sentence fragment depends upon whether it is used intentionally or not, and second, that in an elementary course in composition most instructors assume that a sentence fragment is unintended.

Study carefully the following sentence fragments and the accompanying comments:

A large woman of rather determined attitude who says that she wishes to see you to discuss a matter of great importance. [This is a typical fragment unintended by the writer, who seems to have felt that it is a complete sentence because there are a subject and a predicate in each subordinate clause.]

He finally decided to leave school. Because he was utterly bored with his work and was failing all his courses. [Here the second group of words is an unjustifiable fragment. It is a subordinate clause and should be attached to the main clause without a break of any kind.]

There were books everywhere. Books in the living room, books in the bedroom, books even in the kitchen. [The second group of words is a fragment, but it may be defended on grounds of emphasis. Many writers, however, would have used a comma or colon after *everywhere* and made a single sentence.]

NAME .... SCORE ....

Exercise 14   THE SENTENCE FRAGMENT

Indicate in the space at the right by writing *C* or *F* whether the following groups of words are complete sentences or fragments of sentences. Rewrite any fragment making it a complete sentence.

EXAMPLE: The Grand Canyon National Park located in Arizona.   .....*F*....

The Grand Canyon National Park is located in Arizona.

1. California, a state which attracts many of my friends.   ....

2. The tournament features more than thirty international tennis stars.   ....

3. If you have never painted before.   ....

4. After the play, which was over at ten o'clock.   ....

5. During his illness he never lost his sense of humor.   ....

6. While still a girl living in Apple Valley.   ....

7. Albert studied music with the best teachers of the day.   ....

8. His three marriages, two of which were short-lived.   ....

9. T. S. Eliot, having won an honored position among modern poets.   ....

10. One of the collection's most fascinating books.   ....

11. Be sure that you eat at Ma Hull's in Atlanta.   ....

12. While they were in Michigan, they visited Mackinac Island.   ....

13. Though the characters are well developed.   ....

14. The object of the meeting, which will be short.   ....

15. Attempts have been made to telephone the camp.   ....

16. Charlemagne, the first ruler of the Holy Roman Empire, who died in 814.   ....

17. The small but growing collection of rare stones.   ....

18. An issue that must be faced by the next generation.   ....

19. Alfalfa, one of the oldest crops in the world.   ....

20. During the afternoon we went to a movie.   ....

21. Although the debate over human rights is an ancient one.   ....

22. If you cannot find the book which I told you about.   ....

23. The raven, which is a frequent subject of poetry.   ....

24. These reports, together with Jake's record.   ....

25. Even though the first opera of the season was not well known.   ....

Exercise 15   THE SENTENCE FRAGMENT

Some of the following groups are fragments. Some are fragments and sentences. Some are complete sentences. Rewrite in such a way as to leave no fragments. If the group of words is already a complete sentence, leave it as it is.

EXAMPLE: I enjoyed reading Dickens's novel. Because it carried me from one adventure to another.

I enjoyed reading Dickens's novel because it carried me from one adventure to another.

1. When I got home. I looked everywhere for my riding boots.

2. Mike missed his ride. Because he was not ready.

3. When the play was over and we left the theater.

4. The man-made lake almost complete. Which will be stocked with fish.

5. Walking to the pitcher's mound. The team's manager said something to the veteran pitcher.

6. I plan to leave the city. After I visit the Smithsonian tomorrow.

7. Ted bought fifty acres in the country. In order to breed Thoroughbred horses.

8. The Mount Rushmore Memorial with its carved heads of Washington, Jefferson, Lincoln, and Theodore Roosevelt. It attracts many visitors.

9. I recently finished reading a biography of Flannery O'Connor. A great American author.

10. Mt. Everest, which is the world's highest mountain. It is located in Tibet.

11. Because of the beautiful scenery, we will travel U.S. Highway 81 on our way to Vermont.

12. The city workers' strike finally ending. The workers returned to their jobs.

13. An exchange student using a ham radio. He helped save the Panamanian vessel *Rhinoceros.*

14. Winning the Pulitzer Prize in Letters in 1940, John Steinbeck. The book was *The Grapes of Wrath.*

15. I was late for the Standard Federal Board meeting. My clock having stopped.

Exercise 16   THE SENTENCE FRAGMENT

Complete or revise the following sentence fragments in such a way as to make complete sentences.

EXAMPLE: Cranberries, a treat at any time and always served with our Thanksgiving turkey.

Cranberries, a treat at any time, are always served with our Thanksgiving turkey.

1. As we strolled down the winding path.

2. Travelers on I-75 who have the time and the inclination.

3. When my brother visited the Bowdoin campus.

4. In remote places people who enjoy eating venison.

5. By choosing this horrible back road.

6. Giles and Judy, who are both deaf and who won the clogging contest last year.

7. The reason Marilyn moved to Augusta.

8. *Tiger at the Gates*, written by Jean Giraudoux and a play about the futility of war.

9. Our rock group which includes seven members: a singer, two guitarists, an organist, a trumpeter, a drummer, and an arranger.

10. The old man, reclining in a lounge chair while reading Richard Connell's "The Most Dangerous Game."

Verbals 4

Difficulty in recognizing verbs is often encountered because certain verb forms which function partly as verbs and partly as other parts of speech are confused with sentence verbs. (The *sentence verb* is the verb that states something about the subject, one capable of completing a statement.) These other verb forms are made from verbs but also perform the function of nouns, adjectives, or adverbs. In other words, they constitute a sort of half-verb. They are called **verbals**. The three verbals forms are the **gerund**, the **participle**, and the **infinitive**.

4a Verbals and Sentence Verbs

It is important that you distinguish between the use of a particular verb form as a verbal and its use as a main verb in a sentence. An illustration of the different uses of the verb form *running* will help you to make this distinction:

> *Running* every day is good exercise. [*Running* is a **gerund** and is the subject of the verb *is.*]
>
> *Running* swiftly, he caught the bandit. [*Running* is a **participle** and modifies the pronoun *he.*]
>
> The boy *is running* down the street. [*Is running* is the **sentence verb**. It is formed by using the present participle with the auxiliary verb *is.*]

It must be emphasized that *a verbal cannot take the place of a sentence verb* and that *any group of words containing a verbal but no sentence verb is a sentence fragment:*

> The boy *running* [A sentence fragment.]
>
> *To face* an audience [A sentence fragment.]
>
> The boy *running* up the steps is Charles. [A complete sentence.]
>
> *To face* an audience was a great effort for me. [A complete sentence.]

The following table shows the tenses and voices in which verbals appear:

GERUNDS AND PARTICIPLES

Tense	Active Voice	Passive Voice
Present	doing	being done
Past		done (This form applies only to participles.)
Present Perfect	having done	having been done
Progressive Present Perfect	having been doing	

INFINITIVES

Tense	Active Voice	Passive Voice
Present	to do	to be done
Present Perfect	to have done	to have been done
Progressive Present	to be doing	
Progressive Present Perfect	to have been doing	

4b   The Gerund

A **gerund** is a verbal used as a noun and in its present tense always ends in *-ing*. Like a noun, a gerund is used as a subject, a complement, an object of a preposition, or an appositive. Do not confuse the gerund with the present participle, which has the same form but is used as an adjective:

> *Planning* the work carefully required a great deal of time. [*Planning* is a gerund used as subject of the sentence.]
>
> She was not to blame for *breaking* the vase. [*Breaking* is a gerund used as object of the preposition *for*.]
>
> I appreciated your *taking* time to help me. [*Taking* is a gerund used as direct object of *appreciated*.]
>
> His unselfish act, *giving* Marty his coat, plainly showed Ed's generosity. [*Giving* is a gerund used as the appositive of *act*.]

In the sentences above you will note examples of gerunds functioning as nouns but also taking objects as verbs do. In the first sentence the gerund *planning* is used as the subject of the verb *required. Planning* itself, however, is completed by the object *work* and is modified by the adverb *carefully*. This dual functioning of the gerund is apparent in the other three sentences as well.

It is important to remember a rule concerning the modification of gerunds: Always use the possessive form of a noun or pronoun before a gerund. Because gerunds are nouns, their modifiers, other than the adverbial ones just mentioned, must be adjectival; therefore, the possessive form, which has adjectival function, is the correct modifier:

Mr. Bridges was surprised at *Doug's* offering him the motorboat.

NOT

Mr. Bridges was surprised at Doug offering him the motorboat.

4c The Participle

A **participle** is a verbal used as an adjective. The present participle is formed by adding *-ing* to the verb: *do – doing.* Again, remember not to confuse the gerund and the present participle, which have the same form but do not function similarly. The past participle is formed in various ways. It may end in *-ed, -d, -t,* or *-n: talk – talked, hear – heard, feel – felt, know – known.* It may also be formed by a change of vowel: *sing – sung.*

> The baby, *wailing* pitifully, refused to be comforted. [*Wailing* is a present participle. It modifies *baby.*]
>
> The *broken* doll can be mended. [*Broken* is a past participle, passive voice. It modifies *doll.*]
>
> An old coat, *faded* and *torn,* was her only possession. [*Faded* and *torn* are past participles, passive voice, modifying *coat.*]
>
> *Having been warned,* the man was sent on his way. [*Having been warned* is the present perfect participle, passive voice. It modifies *man.*]

Like the gerund, the participle may have a complement and adverbial modifiers. In the sentence *Wildly waving a red flag, he ran down the track,* the participle *waving* has the object *flag* and the adverbial modifier *wildly.*

4d The Infinitive

An **infinitive** is a verbal consisting of the simple form of the verb preceded by *to* and used as a noun, an adjective, or an adverb:

> *To err* is human. [*To err* is used as a noun, the subject of *is.*]
>
> He wanted *to go* tomorrow. [*To go* is used as a noun, the object of the verb *wanted.*]
>
> He had few books *to read.* [*To read* is used as an adjective to modify the noun *books.*]
>
> Frank seemed eager *to go.* [*To go* is used as an adverb to modify the adjective *eager.*]
>
> She rode fast *to escape* her pursuers. [*To escape* is used as an adverb to modify the verb *rode.*]

Sometimes the word *to* is omitted:

> Susan helped *carry* the packages. [*To* is understood before the verb *carry.* (*To*) carry is used as an adverb to modify the verb *helped.*]

NOTE: An adverbial infinitive can frequently be identified if the phrase "in order" can be placed before it, as in *Katy paid ten dollars* (in order) *to get good seats at the play.*

Like the gerund and the participle, the infinitive may have a complement and adverbial modifiers:

> He did not want *to cut the grass yesterday.* [The infinitive *to cut* has the object *grass* and the adverbial modifier *yesterday.*]

Exercise 17   VERBS AND VERBALS

In the following sentences identify each *italicized* expression by writing on the line at the right.

V if it is a verb,   *Part* if it is a participle,
Ger if it is a gerund,   *Inf* if it is an infinitive.

EXAMPLE: I refuse *to eat* snails.   *Inf*

1. My pet hates are *skiing* and *hiking*.   ....

2. He stood at the window, *watching* the Founders' Day parade.   ....

3. Hugh's first job *was* washing pots and pans in Peoria, Illinois.   ....

4. The lion kills its prey by *choking* it with a throat bite.   ....

5. The weather in Maine *was* predictably cold.   ....

6. What underdeveloped countries need is *to increase* their technological capacity.   ....

7. The decision *to issue* new guidelines was not an easy one.   ....

8. The panoramic view was *breathtaking*.   ....

9. All visitors to Skidaway Island have the opportunity *to see* dozens of sea creatures.   ....

10. *Facing* the crowd, John Denver began singing "Country Road."   ....

11. *To master* a foreign language takes time and intelligence.   ....

12. We are faced with the necessity of *forming* international ocean management policies.   ....

13. I wanted *to eat* supper at Deacon Burton's.   ....

14. She always *kept* her tank full of gas.   ....

15. They said that he died of a *broken* heart.   ....

16. We plan *to spend* the summer in London.   ....

17. The leader, *deceived* by his advisors, was doomed to fail.   ....

18. Jeff enjoyed both *camping* and mountain *climbing.*   ....

19. *Have* you *told* our secret?   ....

20. Moderation is a difficult word *to define.*   ....

21. You can expect the chorus *to play* an important role in the opera <u>Carmen</u>.   ....

22. The *opening* scene of <u>Star Wars</u> is overwhelming.   ....

23. *Learning* can be exciting.   ....

24. I *have known* him for many years.   ....

25. *Are* you willing to accept the responsibility?   ....

Exercise 18   GERUNDS

In the following sentences underline each gerund. Copy the gerund on the first line at the right. On the second line write

         S if the gerund is the subject of the verb,
         PN if the gerund is the predicate nominative,
         DO if the gerund is the direct object of the verb,
         OP if the gerund is the object of the preposition.

	GERUND	FUNCTION
EXAMPLE: The children enjoyed <u>playing</u> soccer.	*playing*	*DO*
1. Selecting a career is not easy.		
2. We heard about your winning first prize.		
3. Gathering blackberries was a family venture.		
4. To be successful requires planning.		
5. What are her chances of recovering her sight?		
6. His greatest weakness was wasting his time.		
7. After a week of dieting, I had lost three pounds.		
8. Reading a play well requires an active imagination.		
9. Intelligent questioning of cultural values is the hallmark of a scholar.		
10. His reason was overshadowed by the importance of winning.		
11. Angie's summer pastime was reading the poetry of Emily Dickinson.		
12. Mary Ann's responsibility included training all new cadets.		
13. The New York model discovered new ways of standing and moving.		

14. Can't you make a decision without asking for my opinion? ....

15. Riding with Eric is never dull. ....

16. This summer I am enjoying bird-watching. ....

17. His job on the assembly line consists of tightening bolts. ....

18. He continued experimenting with dangerous drugs. ....

19. Living in the country offers new experiences daily. ....

20. I heard the crying of a child. ....

21. By working late, we finished the float on time. ....

22. Jane's job was mowing the grass. ....

23. Hunting down the criminal became an intriguing challenge. ....

24. She began training for the Olympics when she was eight years old. ....

25. Rushing through dinner was not my idea. ....

26. Chris enjoyed masquerading as a secret agent. ....

27. The Europeans understand the art of eating. ....

28. Eating too fast is an American way of life. ....

29. After years of testing, the product was approved. ....

30. Government spending has reached the point of absurdity. ....

Exercise 19   PARTICIPLES

Underline the participle(s) in each of the following sentences, and then write in the space at the right the word which the participle modifies.

EXAMPLE: I have always been afraid of <u>haunted</u> houses.   ....*houses*..........

1. The torn and uprooted trees showed the power of the wind.   ....

2. The child was aware of the flashing lights.   ....

3. Her wrecked car sat in the driveway for a week.   ....

4. The text of the completed novel was never found.   ....

5. An industrialized society has many problems to solve.   ....

6. His declining popularity worried the senator.   ....

7. A throbbing headache kept me from attending the Bluegrass Festival in Dodge City.   ....

8. I could not sleep because of the screaming sirens and screeching tires.   ....

9. Jerusalem is one of the most inspiring cities in the world.   ....

10. Alice is looking for a furnished apartment.   ....

11. The frightened puppy hid under the table.   ....

12. Experienced writers know the need for conciseness.   ....

13. Scott tried to protect his broken hand.   ....

14. Christopher Smart is a forgotten eighteenth-century poet.   ....

15. Her demanding attitude made me angry.   ....

16. David's flight, arriving late, circled the airport.   ....

17. The doctor left the room, followed by two nurses.   ....

18. Can the mechanic repair my clogged carburetor?   ....

19. As we entered the room, we sensed impending danger.   ....

20. Having won the tournament, the team celebrated. ....

21. Dorothy prepared a written summary of her view of the meeting. ....

22. White-water canoeing is both exciting and dangerous. ....

23. Lois sprained her ankle playing tennis. ....

24. Do you enjoy eating dried apples? ....

25. All interested students will be given free tickets to the concert. ....

26. Her most recent book, developed from previous lectures, received excellent reviews. ....

27. The little boy, having arrived at camp, was immediately ready to go home. ....

28. The girl standing by the door is my sister. ....

29. Having washed the car, I expected it to rain. ....

30. She answered the want ad announcing the job. ....

Exercise 20　　INFINITIVES

Underline the infinitive in each of the following sentences, and in the space at the right indicate its use in the sentence by writing *N* for noun, *Adj* for adjective, *Adv* for adverb.

EXAMPLE: To fail the Kansas Bar Examination would delay my graduation.　　　*N*
....

1. The purpose of life is to seek knowledge.　　　..........

2. Most political speeches try to affect an audience emotionally.　　　..........

3. No one wants to spend money on junk.　　　..........

4. It is difficult to direct you to my farm.　　　..........

5. We were all sorry to see Ralph go.　　　..........

6. The purpose of our meeting is to elect a president.　　　..........

7. Harold's party was an event to remember.　　　..........

8. Hermann Hesse's *Demian* is an intriguing book to read.　　　..........

9. Coretta was close enough to the speaker to ask a question.　　　..........

10. What did the man want to know?　　　..........

11. To write well requires frequent practice.　　　..........

12. I was eager to meet my blind date.　　　..........

13. Bob wants to cut down the trees and the shrubs in the front yard.　　　..........

14. I have always hoped to tour Australia.　　　..........

15. The committee was ready to recommend her for a distinguished-service award.　　　..........

16. The boy needs to regain his confidence.　　　..........

17. The city is planning to rebuild the inner city area.　　　..........

18. Todd was too sick to attend the dinner party.　　　..........

19. She has the right to refuse his request.　　　..........

20. We will want to discuss the matter further.　　　..........

21. Alexis has tried for years to lose weight. ....

22. Do you really expect to pass without studying? ....

23. He left college to find his place in society. ....

24. Being in a hurry to leave, I forgot my pocketbook. ....

25. Al expects to take a trip to Canada someday. ....

26. The coach did not try to win the game. ....

27. Plans to build a new coliseum are underway. ....

28. To argue with the umpire is a waste of time. ....

29. Ruth wanted to explain the problem briefly. ....

30. The speaker decided to talk informally. ....

NAME .... SCORE ....

Exercise 21   **VERBALS**

In the following sentences underline each verbal. On the first line at the right identify the type of verbal by writing

Ger for gerund, *Part* for participle, *Inf* for infinitive.

On the second line at the right indicate the use of the verbal by writing

Adj for adjective,	*PN* for predicate nominative,
Adv for adverb,	*DO* for direct object,
S for subject,	*OP* for object of a preposition.

	TYPE	**USE**
EXAMPLE: I objected to Jim's <u>playing</u> hockey.	*Ger*	*OP*
1. Before leaving Washington, please give me your new address.	....	....
2. He tried to make a cardboard box look like a suitcase.	....	....
3. We appreciate your accepting our invitation.	....	....
4. Many Americans spend too much time watching television.	....	....
5. Jogging around the pond is the way I begin my day.	....	....
6. The farmer enjoys working the land.	....	....
7. We decided not to buy new furniture until next year.	....	....
8. After knocking on several doors, I finally found my aunt's apartment.	....	....
9. The old man refused to accept the physicians' advice.	....	....
10. The child looked sad and dejected.	....	....
11. Ed resented Jan's driving his sports car.	....	....
12. Walking through the woods, I met a rattlesnake on my path.	....	....
13. Each girl should bring her own camping equipment.	....	....
14. To take your vacation next week, you must complete all your work.	....	....
15. Motorcycle racing is dangerous.	....	....

16. He had a moral obligation to publish his report. ....

17. A truck jackknifed on the turnpike, spilling a load of apples across the highway. ....

18. Marge was anxious to know the verdict. ....

19. They needed a place to practice. ....

20. The increasing popularity of country living poses many problems for big city officials. ....

21. Only you and Bill are able to help him. ....

22. Spinning around on the piano stool, the little boy howled. ....

23. After her Scandinavian tour, she had many experiences to tell. ....

24. The adventurer's only hope was to find a sunken treasure. ....

25. Jessie plans to buy a new Jeep truck next year. ....

Recognizing Phrases 5

A **phrase** is a group of related words, generally having neither subject nor predicate and used as though it were a single word. It cannot make a statement and is therefore not a clause.

A knowledge of the phrase and how it is used will suggest to you ways of diversifying and enlivening your sentences. Variety in using sentences will remedy the monotonous "subject first" habit. For instance, the use of the participial phrase will add life and movement to your style, because the participle is an action word, having the strength of its verbal nature in addition to its function as a modifier.

We classify phrases as **gerund, participial, infinitive, absolute, prepositional,** and **appositive.** The following sentences will show how the same idea may be expressed differently by the use of different kinds of phrases:

> Sue swam daily. She hoped to improve her backstroke. ["Subject first" sentences.]
>
> By *swimming daily*, Sue hoped to improve her backstroke. [Gerund phrase.]
>
> *Swimming daily*, Sue hoped to improve her backstroke. [Participial phrase.]
>
> Sue's only hope of improving her backstroke was *to swim daily*. [Infinitive phrase.]
>
> *With a daily swim* Sue hoped to improve her backstroke. [Prepositional phrase.]

5a The Gerund Phrase

A **gerund phrase** consists of a gerund and any complement or modifiers it may have. The function of the gerund phrase is always that of a noun:

> *Being late for breakfast* is Joe's worst fault. [The gerund phrase is used as the subject of the verb *is*.]
>
> She finally succeeded in *opening the camera*. [The gerund phrase is the object of the preposition *in*.]

Bill hated *driving his golf balls into the lake.* [The gerund phrase is the object of the verb *hated.*]

His hobby, *making furniture,* is enjoyable and useful. [The gerund phrase is an appositive.]

5b   The Participial Phrase

A **participial phrase** consists of a participle and any complement or modifiers it may have. It functions as an adjective:

Disappointed by his best friend, Roger refused to speak to him. [The participial phrase modifies the proper noun *Roger.*]

Having written the letter, Julie set out for the Post Office. [The participial phrase modifies the proper noun *Julie.*]

The boy *standing in the doorway* is the one who asked to borrow our rake. [The participial phrase modifies the noun *boy.*]

PUNCTUATION: Introductory participial phrases are set off by commas. Other participial phrases are also set off by commas unless they are essential to the meaning of the sentence. (See Chapter 19, Section b.)

5c   The Infinitive Phrase

An **infinitive phrase** consists of an infinitive and any complement or modifiers it may have. Infinitives function as adjectives, adverbs, or nouns:

She had a plane *to catch at eight o'clock.* [The infinitive phrase modifies the noun *plane.*]

To be in Mr. Foster's class was *to learn the meaning of discipline.* [The first infinitive phrase is the subject of the verb *was.* The second infinitive phrase is the predicate nominative after the verb *was.*]

Millie left early *to avoid the heavy traffic.* [The infinitive phrase modifies the verb *left.*]

After the night outdoors we were happy *to be warm and dry again.* [The infinitive phrase modifies the adjective *happy.*]

Ted has no plans except *to watch television.* [The infinitive phrase is the object of the preposition *except.*]

We decided *to go for a long walk.* [The infinitive phrase is the direct object of the verb *decided.*]

Her fiancé seems *to be very pleasant.* [The infinitive phrase is the predicate adjective after the verb *seems.*]

PUNCTUATION: Introductory infinitive phrases used as modifiers are set off by commas. (See Chapter 19, Section b.)

5d   The Absolute Phrase

A noun followed by a participle may form a construction grammatically independent of the rest of the sentence. This construction is called an **absolute phrase**. It is never a subject, nor does it modify any word in the sentence, but it is used *absolutely* or independently:

> *The bus having stopped,* the tourists filed out.
>
> *The theater being nearby,* I decided to walk.
>
> I shall do as I please, *all things considered.*

PUNCTUATION: An absolute phrase is always separated from the rest of the sentence by a comma. (See Chapter 19, Section b.)

5e The Prepositional Phrase

A **prepositional phrase** consists of a preposition followed by a noun or pronoun used as its object, together with any modifiers the noun or pronoun may have. The prepositional phrase functions usually as an adjective or an adverb:

> The plan *of the house* is very simple. [The prepositional phrase modifies the noun *plan.*]
>
> The river runs *through rich farmland.* [The prepositional phrase modifies the verb *runs.*]

PUNCTUATION: An introductory prepositional phrase, unless unusually long, is not set off by a comma. (See Chapter 19, Section b.)

5f The Appositive Phrase

An **appositive** is a word or phrase which follows another word and means the same thing. An appositive may be a noun phrase (that is, a noun and its modifiers), a gerund phrase, an infinitive phrase, or a prepositional phrase:

> This book, *a long novel about politics,* will never be a best seller. [Noun phrase used as an appositive.]
>
> Jean knew a way out of her difficulty: *telling the truth.* [Gerund phrase used as an appositive.]
>
> His greatest ambition, *to make a million dollars,* was doomed from the start. [Infinitive phrase used as an appositive.]
>
> The rustler's hideout, *in the old cave by the river,* was discovered by the posse. [Prepositional phrase used as an appositive.]

An appositive may be **essential** (sometimes called **fused**) or **nonessential**; it is essential if it positively identifies that which it renames, frequently by use of a proper noun. Examples of both essential and nonessential appositives occur in the sentences below:

> The Victorian poets *Tennyson and Browning* were outstanding literary spokesmen of their day. [The appositive, *Tennyson and Browning,* identifies *poets* and thus is essential.]
>
> Tennyson and Browning, *two Victorian poets,* were outstanding literary spokesmen of their day. [The appositive, *two Victorian poets,* is nonessential because the poets are already identified by their names.]

PUNCTUATION: An appositive phrase is enclosed with commas unless it is essential. (See Chapter 19, Section b.)

Exercise 22   PHRASES

In each of the sentences below identify the *italicized* phrase by writing in the space at the right

> *Prep* if it is a prepositional phrase,   *Inf* if it is an infinitive phrase,
> *Part* if it is a participial phrase,   *App* if it is an appositive phrase,
> *Ger* if it is a gerund phrase,   *Abs* if it is an absolute phrase.

EXAMPLE: *The rain having stopped,* I plowed the south forty.   *Abs*

1. The silence of the night was cut *by a woman's scream.*   ....

2. *All things considered,* the Dallas Cowboys played a good game.   ....

3. *To provide efficient service* requires tremendous staff effort.   ....

4. The man *standing on the corner* is a foreign agent.   ....

5. *Between these two covers* you will find a spellbinding book.   ....

6. By *establishing residency,* you will be allowed to vote in the next election.   ....

7. The veterans, *scarred by the war*, returned home.   ....

8. I think that *working crossword puzzles* is fun.   ....

9. The Romantic poets *Keats and Byron* lived tragic lives.   ....

10. All employees have been asked *to read the personnel handbook.*   ....

11. We hurried home, *the storm having started.*   ....

12. One night we camped on a sand dune *near the ocean.*   ....

13. My truck, *a 1972 Ford Courier,* has traveled over seventy thousand miles.   ....

14. *Rappelling down the cliff* frightened me my first time.   ....

15. Dr. Alexander, *a university professor,* has an almost unlimited knowledge of Greek literature.   ....

16. The man *wearing the bow tie* is the quarterback's father.   ....

17. The stadium became silent, *the crowd having gone.*   ....

18. *To write effectively* requires clear thinking.   ....

19. Henry had a habit of *locking his keys in the car.*   ....

20. My two hobbies, *fishing and mountain climbing,* take up all my leisure time.   ....

Exercise 23   PHRASES

The sentences in the following exercise contain prepositional, verbal, and appositive phrases. Underline each phrase, and in the space at the right of each sentence show how each phrase is used by writing *Adj* for adjective, *Adv* for adverb, and *N* for noun.

EXAMPLE: The snake moved gracefully <u>through the grass</u>.   *Adv*
                                                                           ....

1. Reid wanted to ride his new bicycle home.   ....

2. The young man driving the Mustang will probably win the race.   ....

3. To avoid the afternoon traffic, we left early.   ....

4. We decided to postpone our trip.   ....

5. Our speaker, a famous writer, will read various popular poems.   ....

6. The attorney for the defendant asked too many embarrassing questions.   ....

7. The two women, carrying their own golf bags, crossed the fairway.   ....

8. Ned tried to control his anger.   ....

9. I enjoy an early morning walk on the beach.   ....

10. Our flight was delayed by the storm.   ....

11. The enemy retreated shortly before dawn.   ....

12. He paused to admire the shiny new cabin cruiser.   ....

13. The man wearing the pinstripe suit is my favorite uncle.   ....

14. Lord Emsworth tried to find an answer which would satisfy his sister.   ....

15. The shy rabbit disappeared into the shrubbery.   ....

16. Making vacation plans is always fun.   ....

17. Constance began playing the piano when she was three years old.   ....

18. Today's assignment is to read Frank O'Connor's "First Confession."   ....

19. Driving an old, fenderless truck did not bother Sally.   ....

20. Steve always did enjoy reading biographies. ....

21. Her failure to appear raised eyebrows. ....

22. Chris tore her dress on the barbed wire. ....

23. To make the table steady, we braced the legs. ....

24. When we visit Pawley's Island, I plan to buy a hammock. ....

25. The old coon dog was lying behind the kitchen stove. ....

Exercise 24   PHRASES

In each of the following sentences underline the phrase. In the first space at the right identify the type of phrase by writing

> *Prep* for prepositional phrase,   *Inf* for infinitive phrase,
> *Part* for participial phrase,   *App* for appositive phrase.
> *Ger* for gerund phrase,

Then indicate in the second space its use by writing *Adj, Adv,* or *N.*

	TYPE	USE
EXAMPLE: Washing the car is not my responsibility.	*Ger*	*N*
1. Her library was filled with books, magazines, and papers.	....	....
2. The man wearing the dark glasses introduced the mysterious lady.	....	....
3. How many books did you read during the summer?	....	....
4. She does not like to be disturbed.	....	....
5. Almost anything would have tasted good to the lost campers.	....	....
6. Watching television is often a pleasant escape.	....	....
7. Having finished his research, Jeff left the library.	....	....
8. Dr. Davis, my mother's doctor, is a very humane woman.	....	....
9. Several new books about World War II have recently been published.	....	....
10. We plan to visit New Orleans this fall.	....	....
11. Our children enjoy gathering the pecans.	....	....
12. Have you read Eugene O'Neill's play *Emperor Jones?*	....	....
13. Giving advice is sometimes dangerous.	....	....
14. To become a college president has always been her goal.	....	....
15. Our visit to the Lake Country was an unforgettable experience.	....	....
16. The young lawyer increased his business by hard work.	....	....

17. Upon the door she hung her new evening dress.   ....

18. Riding her horse is Jan's current pastime.   ....

19. My neighbor plans to plant his fall garden next week.   ....

20. The new player kicked a field goal of sixty yards.   ....

Exercise 25   **PHRASES**

A. Combine the following pairs of sentences, making one sentence a participial phrase. Punctuate each sentence properly.

EXAMPLE: We sat around the campfire. We told tales of the old days.
             Sitting around the campfire, we told tales of the old days.

1. The heirs listened to the reading of the will. Most of the heirs became angry.

2. Tom missed his flight. He spent the night in Chicago.

3. Carlos considered several alternatives. He decided to apply for admission to medical school.

4. The Nathaniel Russell House was built in 1809. It is noted for its floating staircase and grand oval rooms.

5. She completed her research paper early. She had time to proofread it and make corrections.

6. The witness attempted to avoid the attorney's questions. He hesitated frequently.

7. The bat was attracted by the campfire. It frightened all of us.

8. We heard Sue's boisterous laughter. We knew that it was she.

9. Elmer worked diligently. He surpassed those who competed against him.

10. *Shogun* was written by James Clavell. It is a novel about Japan.

B. Combine the following pairs of sentences, making one of the sentences an appositive phrase.

EXAMPLE: Angie is a first-year medical student. She wants to become a surgeon.
            Angie, a first-year medical student, wants to become a surgeon.

1. Bill thinks that regular study is important. He is a Baylor University student.

2. *My Fair Lady* is a musical version of *Pygmalion.* It is an adaptation of Shaw's play about an uneducated Cockney girl.

3. Woodrow Wilson was born December 28, 1856, in Virginia. He was one of our greatest presidents.

4. My brother-in-law is the oldest of the four sons. He is an attorney in Atlanta.

5. Sir Walter Scott's first novel was *Waverly.* It was published in 1814.

6. Adam Tanner is our hockey coach. He will award the Best Player Trophy at the banquet.

7. Charlotte Bronte's most famous novel is *Jane Eyre.* It was published under her pseudonym Currer Bell.

8. My father is a good fisherman. He taught me how to fly-cast.

9. Perseus was a Greek hero. He killed the monster Medusa and saved the life of Andromeda.

10. Cycling was a popular sport during the twenties. It is returning.

Exercise 26   PUNCTUATION OF PHRASES

In the following sentences insert all commas required by the rules stated in Chapter 5. In the blanks write the commas with the words which precede them. When the sentence requires no comma, write *C* in the space.

EXAMPLE: The whistle having been blown˄ the race began.   *blown,*

1. "A Good Man Is Hard to Find" written by Flannery O'Connor is a story of desperate people.   ....

    ....

2. Frances born in Canada did not want to move to Texas.   ....

    ....

3. Driving across town takes at least an hour.   ....

4. Sophocles a Greek dramatist believed that we obtain wisdom through suffering.   ....

    ....

5. All things considered I think that the committee made the right decision.   ....

6. Alarmed by the ambassador's report the President called a meeting of his cabinet.   ....

7. Watching television will dull a person's imagination.   ....

8. The blind girl hearing the crash hesitated before crossing the street.   ....

    ....

9. Taking the doctor's advice we both stopped smoking.   ....

10. To reduce our grocery bill we bought less junk food.   ....

11. Conserving energy is everyone's responsibility.   ....

12. Being an interpreter for the deaf Jimmy has the opportunity to meet people from all walks of life.   ....

13. Constantly finding fault is the mark of a little mind.   ....

14. The boy in the motorcycle accident was traveling too fast.   ....

15. Determined to catch enough fish for supper my brother and nephew set several lines.   ....

16. Beryl having lost her money cut her vacation short.   ....

....

17. *Thanksgiving* a work by Doris Lee is a primitive painting.   ....

....

18. Responding to his young daughter's curiosity he took her for a walk in the woods.   ....

19. Wandering up an unpaved road we found an old mill.   ....

20. The young woman eating alone is a new vice president of the University.   ....

Independent Clauses 6

6a Independent Clauses

A group of words containing a subject and a verb and expressing a complete thought is called a sentence or an **independent clause.** Some groups of words which contain a subject and a verb, however, do not express a complete thought and therefore cannot stand alone as a sentence. Such word groups are dependent on other sentence elements and are called **dependent clauses.**

Sometimes an independent clause stands alone as a sentence. Sometimes two or more independent clauses are combined into one sentence without a connecting word. Then a semicolon is used to connect the independent clauses:

> The day is cold.
> The day is cold; the wind is howling.

Sometimes independent clauses are connected by one of the coordinating conjunctions, *and, but, for, or, nor, so,* and *yet.* As these conjunctions do not subordinate, an independent clause beginning with one of them may stand as a complete sentence. Independent clauses joined by a coordinating conjunction are separated by commas. Therefore, to punctuate correctly, you must distinguish between independent clauses and other kinds of sentence elements joined by coordinating conjunctions. In the following examples note that only independent clauses joined by coordinating conjunctions are separated by commas:

> The day was *dark* and *dreary.* [The conjunction *and* joins two adjectives, *dark* and *dreary.* No comma permitted.]
>
> The fallen tree *blocked* the highway and *delayed* travel. [The conjunction *and* joins the two verbs. No comma permitted.]
>
> She ran *up the steps* and *into the house.* [The conjunction *and* joints two phrases. No comma permitted.]

Mrs. Brown caught the fish, and *her husband cooked them.* [The conjunction *and* connects two independent clauses, and these are separted by a comma.]

Sometimes two independent clauses are connected by a **conjunctive,** or **transitional, adverb** such as one of the following:

however	moreover	nevertheless	therefore
then	accordingly	otherwise	thus
hence	besides	consequently	

A semicolon is necessary before any of these words beginning a second clause. After the longer *conjunctive adverbs* a comma is generally used:

We drove all day; *then* at sundown we began to look for a place to camp.

It rained during the afternoon; *consequently,* our trip to the mountains had to be postponed.

NOTE:. Conjunctive adverbs can be distinguished from subordinating conjunctions by the fact that the *adverbs* can be shifted to a later position in the sentence, whereas the *conjunctions* cannot:

It rained during the afternoon; our trip to the mountains, *consequently,* had to be postponed.

SUMMARY OF PUNCTUATION: From the foregoing discussion and examples we can establish the following rules for the punctuation of independent clauses:

1. *Two independent clauses connected by a coordinating conjunction are separated by a comma:*

   Our goat chewed up the morning paper, *and* Father is angry.

   You should call Hank tonight, *for* he is all alone.

2. *Two independent clauses which are not connected by a coordinating conjunction are separated by a semicolon.* Remember that this rule also holds true when the second clause begins with a conjunctive adverb:

   Philip is quite strong; he is much stronger than I.

   We both wanted to go to the toboggan race; *however,* Mother had asked us to be home by six.

3. *A semicolon is used to separate independent clauses which are joined by a coordinating conjunction but which are heavily punctuated with commas internally:*

   Harry, George, and Kitty went to Sky Valley for skiing; but Tony and I were too tired to go.

4. *Short independent clauses, when used in a series with a coordinating conjunction preceding the final clause, may be separted by commas:*

   The audience was seated, the lights were dimmed, and the curtain was raised.

   NOTE: A series consists of at least three elements.

6b   The Comma Splice

Use of a comma between two independent clauses not joined by a coordinating conjunction (Rule 2), is a major error called the **comma splice** (This term comes from the idea of splicing or "patching" together two clauses which should be more strongly separated.):

COMMA SPLICE: I enjoyed his company, I do not know that he enjoyed mine.

CORRECTION: I enjoyed his company, but I do not know that he enjoyed mine. (Using Rule 1)

I enjoyed his company; I do not know that he enjoyed mine. (Using Rule 2)

OR

I enjoyed his company; however, I do not know that he enjoyed mine. (Using Rule 2)

6c The Run-together Sentence

The **run-together sentence** results from omitting punctuation between two independent clauses not joined by a conjunction. Basically the error is the same as that of the comma splice: it shows ignorance of sentence structure:

Twilight had fallen it was dark under the old oak tree near the house.

When you read the sentence just given, you have difficulty in getting the meaning at first because the ideas are run together. Now consider the following sentence:

Twilight had fallen, it was dark under the old oak tree near the house.

The insertion of the comma is not a satisfactory remedy, for the sentence now contains a comma splice. There are, however, four approved devices for correcting the run-together sentence and the comma splice:

1. Connect two independent clauses by a comma and a coordinating conjunction if the two clauses are logically of equal importance:

Twilight had fallen, and it was dark under the old oak tree near the house.

2. Connect two independent clauses by a semicolon if they are close enough in thought to make one sentence and you want to omit the conjunction:

Twilight had fallen; it was dark under the old oak tree near the house.

3. Write the two independent clauses as separate sentences if they need separate emphasis:

Twilight had fallen. It was dark under the old oak tree near the house.

4. Subordinate one of the independent clauses:

When twilight had fallen, it was dark under the old oak tree near the house.

THE COMMA SPLICE AND THE RUN-
TOGETHER SENTENCE

Mark correct sentences with a *C*, run-together sentences with an *R*, and sentences containing a
comma splice with *CS*.

EXAMPLE: The Studio Theater is small, consequently, we should arrive early.   *CS*

1. Norma's pet snake sneaked out of the house this morning it has not returned.   ....

2. The schooner was crushed by the force of the wave, all aboard were miraculously
saved.   ....

3. Although I enjoy shopping for Christmas presents, buying each relative a gift
is expensive.   ....

4. The artist had spent the entire day with a collector, therefore, he wanted
to spend the evening alone.   ....

5. Scuba diving is his favorite sport each year he takes a Caribbean vacation.   ....

6. We ate our meals in the pine-walled dining room, which was noisy
with the chatter of hungry guests.   ....

7. The tide is in, now we have a comfortable breeze.   ....

8. We spent the day sunbathing on the beach I got sunburned.   ....

9. She wanted to major in electrical engineering, accordingly, she applied to
Georgia Tech.   ....

10. Although bears are numerous in Smoky Mountain Park, they seldom attack
people.   ....

11. Many of the barns of Lancaster County are disappearing, new agricultural
methods no longer require the old-fashioned barns.   ....

12. We are having dinner at Custy's restaurant, it is impossible to describe everything
offered on his buffet.   ....

13. I enjoyed reading Schumacher's *Small Is Beautiful* because of the author's
novel approach to economics.   ....

14. Sandra was sorry to see the short days of winter come she did not have time to
work in her garden before dark.   ....

15. Chaucer is frequently called the father of English poetry; he is the author of *The Canterbury Tales.*   ....

16. In the story the hero successfully returns home, however, he soon yearns for new adventures.   ....

17. On rainy days we play dominoes I always lose.   ....

18. Every fruit grower fears a late spring frost which would destroy his crop.   ....

19. Heavy snows prevented our hike, hence, we spent the evening telling stories of our children.   ....

20. The College of William and Mary was founded in 1693, it is recognized for its academic excellence.   ....

Exercise 28   THE COMMA SPLICE AND THE RUN-TOGETHER SENTENCE

Mark correct sentences with a *C*, run-together sentences with an *R*, and sentences containing a comma splice with *CS*.

EXAMPLE: Ireland loves folklore, for this reason many popular festivals are held.   ..*CS*..

1. *The End of the Dream* is a thought-provoking novel by Philip Wylie.   ....

2. Mrs. Smith made me a birdhouse, she also made me a feeder.   ....

3. I decided in August to attend college therefore, I encountered several obstacles.   ....

4. The White House is an American showplace; it contains beautiful antiques and gifts from foreign dignitaries.   ....

5. The bank agreed to our paying the note late, thus we received an extension of time.   ....

6. There are many ways to solve a problem everyone thinks his way is the only one.   ....

7. The ambassador's plane landed at the airport on time, she was met by the British Embassy's limousine.   ....

8. You are philosophical about your failures, so you will be able to learn from them.   ....

9. Ronnie has invited his roommates to the country for the weekend they plan to fish and to hunt.   ....

10. Howard knows the fine points of the game, he, therefore, rarely loses.   ....

11. After his speech the Dean received a standing ovation.   ....

12. It looked like rain this morning, so I took my umbrella.   ....

13. Bring your tentative schedule to me I am your advisor.   ....

14. News concerning violent crimes always makes the headlines, however, stories of quiet courage seldom make news.   ....

15. The Industrial Revolution enabled most people to enjoy comforts and conveniences which were only dreamed of by previous generations.   ....

16. Jerry's speech was not particularly convincing, however, it did last an hour and a half.   ....

17. Mt. Everest is the world's highest mountain, it is located in Tibet.   ....

18. Harvey looked inquiringly at the stranger and waited for him to say something.   ....

19. The old mountaineer sat fiddling softly it was past time for him to go to bed.   ....

20. The professor paused a moment for comments from the class none of the students responded.   ....

Exercise 29   PUNCTUATION OF INDEPENDENT CLAUSES

In the following sentences insert all necessary commas and semicolons. In the space at the right write the correct punctuation mark with the word which precedes it. If the sentence is correct, write *C* in the space.

EXAMPLE: We discovered the entrance to the cave but Tim and Mary were afraid to explore it.   *cave,*

1. Politicians spend their time getting votes statesmen spend their time determining the will of the people.   ....

2. I am sorry that I disagree with your interpretation of the story however, I am the author.   ....

3. To participate in the Honors Day program, a student must be in the upper ten percent of her class you are not eligible.   ....

4. It was nearly dark when we got home and we were too exhausted to cut the grass.   ....

5. Carol has finished her year of internship but she has four more years of specialization.   ....

6. The judge was not satisfied with the testimony of the witnesses he called each of them back for further questioning.   ....

7. The house that Nevin built is beautiful but small.   ....

8. Jimmy and Angie get up early and dress quickly they catch the first school bus.   ....

9. We were required to take a physical examination before we could join the biking club.   ....

10. Jessica's children have frequently exposed her to measles but she has never had it.   ....

11. The professor contrasted the Greeks' praise of the individual with the Romans' praise of accomplishments.   ....

12. The afternoon passed rapidly and all too soon it was time to go back to the hotel.   ....

13. We are leaving for Washington tomorrow morning therefore, I will be unable to see you before I leave.   ....

14. The price of each dinner included a soup, salad, entree, and dessert we decided not to think about calories.   ....

15. Bradford Academy was incorporated in 1820, it was one of the first tuition-free coeducational schools in Vermont.   ....

16. The weather is very cold in the mountains, so we will need to take our blankets.   ....

17. The tide is out we can walk along the shore.   ....

18. Too many people confuse a college degree with a college education.   ....

19. Juanita has the highest grade point average in her class in spite of being blind.   ....

20. I realize that each of you has a busy schedule, nevertheless, I hope you will come to the county fair.   ....

Dependent Clauses 7

Any clause beginning with a subordinating word like *what, that, who, which, when, since, before, after,* or *if* is a **dependent clause**. Dependent clauses, like phrases, function as grammatical units in a sentence—that is, as nouns, adjectives, and adverbs:

> I went to school.   }   [Both clauses are independent.]
> Too much time had elapsed.   }
>
> *When I went to school,* I studied my lessons. [The first clause is subordinate.]
>
> *Since too much time had elapsed,* she remained at home. [The first clause is subordinate.]

In the last two sentences *I studied my lessons* and *she remained at home* are complete statements. But the clauses *When I went to school* and *Since too much time had elapsed* do not express complete thoughts. They depend upon the independent statements to complete their meanings. Both of these dependent clauses function as adverbs.

7a Noun Clauses

A **noun clause** is a dependent clause used as a noun, that is, as a subject, complement, object of a preposition, or appositive. Noun clauses are usually introduced by *that, what, why, whether, who, which,* or *how.* Some of these introductory words can introduce both noun and adjective clauses, since the function of the whole clause in the sentence, and not its introductory word, determines its classification. Most sentences containing noun clauses differ from those containing adjective and adverbial clauses in that with the clause removed they are no longer complete sentences:

> Your *plan* is interesting. [The subject is the noun *plan.*]
>
> *What you intend to do* [your plan] is interesting. [The italicized noun clause is the subject of the verb *is.* Notice that the noun *plan* can be substituted for the clause.]

Tell me *what you intend to do* [your plan]. [The italicized noun clause is the direct object of the verb *tell*.]

That is *what you intend to do* [your plan]. [The italicized noun clause is a predicate nominative.]

I am interested in *what you intend to do* [your plan]. [The italicized noun clause is the object of the preposition *in*.]

The fact *that he had not told the truth soon became apparent*. [The italicized noun clause is in apposition with the noun *fact*.]

PUNCTUATION: Noun clauses used as non-essential appositives are set off by commas.

7b Adjective Clauses

An **adjective clause** is a dependent clause which modifies a noun or pronoun. The common connective words used to introduce adjective clauses are the relative pronouns *who* (and its inflected forms *whom* and *whose*), *which*, *that*, and relative adverbs like *where, when,* and *why*. (*Where* and *when* can introduce all three kinds of clauses.)

The italicized clauses in the following sentences are all adjective clauses:

She is a woman *who is respected by everyone.*

Mr. Johnson, *whose son attends the University,* is our friend.

He saw the place *where he was born.*

It was a time *when money did not count.*

I know the reason *why I failed the course.*

Adjective clauses are classified as **essential** (restrictive) and **nonessential** (non-restrictive).

An *essential* clause, as its name indicates, is necessary in a sentence, for it identifies or points out a certain person or thing; a *nonessential* clause adds information about the word it modifies, but it is not essential in pointing out or identifying a certain person or thing:

Thomas Jefferson, *who was born on the frontier,* became President. [The name *Thomas Jefferson* has identified the person, and the italicized clause is not essential.]

A person *who loves to read* will never be lonely. [The italicized adjective clause is essential in identifying a particular kind of person.]

My father, *who was a country boy,* has lived in the city for years. [Since a person has only one father, an identifying clause is not essential.]

The girl *by whom I sat in class* is an honor student. [The italicized adjective clause is essential to the identification of *girl*.]

To determine whether an adjective clause is essential. you may apply this test: read the sentence leaving out the adjective clause and see whether the removal omits necessary identification. Try this test on the following sentence:

Jet pilots, *who work under a great deal of stress,* must stay in excellent physical condition.

You will see that the removal of the adjective clause does not change the basic meaning of the sentence. The italicized adjective clause is, therefore, nonessential.

Now read the following sentence, leaving out the italicized adjective clause:

Jet pilots *who are not in excellent physical condition* should not be allowed to fly.

If the adjective clause of this sentence is removed, the statement is not at all what the writer meant to say. The adjective clause is, therefore, essential.

PUNCTUATION: Nonessential adjective clauses are set off from the rest of the sentence by commas. (See Chapter 19, Section b.)

7c Adverbial Clauses

An **adverbial clause** is a dependent clause that functions exactly as if it were an adverb. Like an adverb it modifies a verb, an adjective, an adverb, or the whole idea expressed in the sentence's independent clause; e.g., *As luck would have it,* we missed his telephone call.

An adverbial clause is used to show *time, place, cause, purpose, result, condition, concession, manner,* or *comparison.* Its first word is a subordinating conjunction. Common subordinating conjunctions and their uses are listed below:

1. Time (*when, before, since, as, while, until, after, whenever*)

   I will stay *until you come.*
   When the whistle blew, the laborer stopped.

2. Place (*where, wherever, whence, whither*)

   He went *where no one had ever set foot before.*
   Wherever you go, I will go too.

3. Cause (*because, since, as*)

   Since I had no classes on Saturday, I went home.
   Because he was afraid of being late, Bob ran all the way.

4. Purpose (*in order that, so that, that*)

   My family made many sacrifices *so that I could have an education.*
   Men work *that they may eat.*

5. Result (*so . . . that, such . . . that*)

   The weather was *so* cold *that I decided not to walk to school.*

6. Condition (*if, unless*)

   You will hurt your hand *if you are not careful.*
   Unless you apply at once, your name will not be considered.

7. Concession (*though, although*)

   Although she had no money, she was determined to go to college.

8. Manner (*as, as if, as though*)

   She looked *as though she wanted to laugh.*
   Do *as you like,* but take the consequences.

9. Comparison (*as, than*)

   He is older *than his brother.*
   He is as tall *as his brother.*

PUNCTUATION: Introductory adverbial clauses are always set off by commas:

> *Although he had tests to take and a term paper to write,* he went home for the weekend.
>
> *While I was eating lunch,* I had a phone call from my brother.

7d   Kinds of Sentences

For the purpose of varying style and avoiding monotony, you may need to be able to distinguish the four basic types of sentences. According to the number and kind of clauses (phrases do not affect sentence type), sentences may be grouped into four types: **simple, compound, complex,** and **compound-complex.**

1. A **simple** sentence is a single independent clause; it has one subject and one predicate. But it may have as a subject more than one noun or pronoun and as a predicate more than one verb:

> Robert has a new car. [Single subject and single predicate.]
>
> *Robert* and his *brother* have a new car. [There is one verb, *have,* but the subject consists of two nouns.]
>
> Robert *washed* and *polished* his new car on Sunday. [There is one subject, *Robert,* but two verbs.]
>
> *Robert* and his *brother washed* and *polished* their new car. [The subject consists of two nouns, *Robert* and *brother*; and the predicate consists of two verbs, *washed* and *polished.*]

2. A **compound** sentence contains at least two independent clauses and no dependent clause:

> Mary likes the mountains, but Jackie prefers the seashore.
>
> A lamp was lighted in the house, the happy family was talking together, and supper was waiting.

3. A **complex** sentence contains only one independent clause and one or more dependent clauses (the dependent clauses are in italics):

> The toy truck *that you gave Molly for her birthday* is broken.
>
> *Why he refused to contribute to the fund* we do not know.

4. A **compound-complex** sentence has at least two independent clauses and one or more dependent clauses (the independent clauses are in italics):

> *My friend was offended by my attitude,* and *I was sorry* that she was hurt.
>
> *We spent the morning looking for the home of the woman* who paints landscapes, but *we were unable to find it.*

Exercise 30   CLAUSES

In the following sentences underline each dependent clause. In the space at the right, write *Adj* if the clause is an adjective clause, *Adv* if it is an adverbial clause, and *N* if it is a noun clause. If the sentence contains no dependent clause, leave the space blank.

EXAMPLE: Will those students who are candidates for the Bachelor of Arts degree
please rise.   *Adj*
....

1. My father insisted that David complete his secondary education in England.   ....

2. What I have read on his application form is all that I know about him.   ....

3. If I had time to read a book, I would reread Tolstoy's *War and Peace.*   ....

4. Dean did not share the easygoing attitude of the sportsmen who romanticized
the hunt.   ....

5. An analysis was made of the information furnished by the agent
before it was sent to headquarters.   ....

6. ~~~~~~~~wished desperately that she had not asked the question.   ....

7. After fifty hours of instruction she was a full-fledged pilot.   ....

8. As she ended her speech, she was almost confident again.   ....

9. The man with the mustache pressed Adam for an answer.   ....

10. Although I never knew much about my father, I think of him often.   ....

11. Life is never simple for anyone except those who refuse to face it.   ....

12. If I had worked all day in the factory, I could not have been more exhausted.   ....

13. Sheila is older than her sister.   ....

14. Mr. Hoffer, whose family lives in Germany, will be our guest this weekend.   ....

15. Unless you leave immediately, you will miss your train.   ....

16. You will be surprised at how simply one can live.   ....

17. He watched her thoughtfully as she walked across the room.   ....

18. When we were seniors in high school, we read *As You Like It* and *Macbeth*. ....

19. As soon as the poet walked in, the audience stood. ....

20. During the first months of World War II, secrecy was our only defense. ....

21. What seems most evident to me is Richard's failure to understand the problem. ....

22. A strange bird call echoed through the trees. ....

23. Once in the woods, she stopped and listened again. ....

24. When the door opened, a white-haired woman entered the room carrying a gun in her hand. ....

25. The explanation which she had given them seemed too horrible to be true. ....

Exercise 31   CLAUSES

Give the function of each of the *italicized* clauses by writing the proper abbreviation in the space at the right:

> *S* for subject of a verb,   *OP* for object of a preposition,
> *DO* for direct object,   *Adj* for adjective modifier,
> *PN* for predicate nominative,   *Adv* for adverbial modifier.

EXAMPLE: Hermann Hesse, *who was awarded both the Goethe Prize and the Nobel Prize,* was a writer with a pronounced sense of justice.   *Adj*

1. The truth is *that I have lost interest in the course.*   ....

2. *While he was searching the archives of the village,* Alex found a forgotten letter written by Napoleon.   ....

3. *That our environment cannot bear unlimited burdens* is a fact which we cannot escape.   ....

4. Visitors to the museum see the technological changes *which have taken place in the field of transportation.*   ....

5. The senator did not have the slightest idea of *how the poor lived or suffered.*   ....

6. We did not know *what the test was going to cover.*   ....

7. *Because the microphone was not working,* the audience had difficulty hearing the speaker.   ....

8. Did you ever dream *that you would live in Sydney?*   ....

9. The rocket was thoroughly tested *before it was launched.*   ....

10. *What one desires* is sometimes hard to get.   ....

11. That model is *what we plan to build next year.*   ....

12. My neighbors suggested *how I should plant my garden.*   ....

13. Agnes is two years younger *than Hugh.*   ....

14. Well, because of *what you said* a discussion will be unnecessary.   ....

15. The photographer *who was hired to take our wedding pictures* forgot to put film in the camera.   ....

16. *That Jeff had neglected studying his calculus* was obvious to everyone in his class.   ....

17. *If you are going to be browsing in a bookstore,* please buy me *Bramble Bush* by Karl N. Llewellyn.   ....

18. *After Juliet had apparently died,* Romeo took his own life.   ....

19. I suppose *that we cannot change your mind.*   ....

20. His being admitted to college depended on *how well he did on the Scholastic Aptitude Test.*   ....

21. My father, *who loves to cook,* bakes bread every Saturday.   ....

22. *If you are not here on time,* we will leave you.   ....

23. Most of the paintings *which are now on exhibit* represent the Hudson River school of art.   ....

24. *Because I enjoy living close to nature,* I bought a farm last year.   ....

25. Ted said *that his sister is planning to work in Dallas this summer.*   ....

26. The wind was blowing so hard *that I had to move inside to finish my letters.*   ....

Exercise 32   REVIEW OF CLAUSES

In the following sentences enclose the dependent clauses in parentheses. In the space at the right indicate the number of independent and dependent clauses in each sentence. Be able to tell the function of each of the dependent clauses. (Note that some sentences may not contain a dependent clause.)

	IND.	DEP.
EXAMPLE: Finally, Albert confessed (that he did not remember) (where Nancy lived.)	*1*	*2*
1. I wish that I could go with you.	....	....
2. If I should hem my slacks which I bought on sale, I would have three new outfits.	....	....
3. When she was a little girl in Los Angeles, she wanted to become an archaeologist who would travel to ancient lands.	....	....
4. Charlotte was twelve years old when her parents moved to America.	....	....
5. If Don, who is the team's captain, cannot inspire the team, perhaps the coach can.	....	....
6. I was surprised to learn that Della is not coming.	....	....
7. In the doorway appeared Haskins, his hair soaking wet, his clothes dirty and torn.	....	....
8. To understand a work of literature, one must study the times in which it was written and the author who wrote it.	....	....
9. The names of those who have passed the final examination will be posted on the bulletin board in the Dean's office.	....	....
10. Gary, who is a university student, is interested in electronics, because the field offers excellent opportunities.	....	....
11. Whoever was questioned appeared cautious and gave vague responses.	....	....
12. That is the young man who I think won the contest.	....	....
13. On the way home Roy punctured both of his tires, and we had to pick him up.	....	....

14. After listening to both speakers, I tried to decide which had presented the better argument.   ....

15. That Al was not given a fair trial is his attorney's main basis for appeal.   ....

16. Jane wanted to be a physician, but her parents wanted her to be a teacher.   ....

17. Devil's Island, which is eight miles off the coast of French Guiana, is the site of a former French penal colony.   ....

18. Whose music do you like better, Bach's or Mozart's?   ....

19. The department head wanted to know how many students are in each class.   ....

20. If we win this game, we will go to the Sugar Bowl.   ....

21. Eugene O'Neill, a famous American playwright, wrote *Long Day's Journey Into Night.*   ....

22. I wish that I had time for a nap.   ....

23. Jeff did not know how he should answer the question.   ....

24. Because the woman had a criminal record, she had difficulty getting a job.   ....

25. If the book were mine, I would make notes in the margin, but it belongs to my roommate, who does not write in her books.   ....